Home Education in Historical Perspective

This book is the first publication to devote serious attention to the history of home education in Britain from the late eighteenth to the early twentieth century. It brings together work by historians, literary scholars and current practitioners who shed new light on the history of home-schooling in the UK both as a practice and as a philosophy. The six historical case studies point to the significance of domestic instruction in the past, and uncover the ways in which changing family forms have affected understandings of the purpose, form and content of education. At the same time, they uncover the ways in which families and individuals adapted to the expansion of formalised schooling. The final article – by philosopher and Elective Home Education practitioner and theorist Richard Davies – uncovers the ways in which the historical analysis can illuminate our understanding of contemporary education. As a whole, the volume offers stimulating insights into the history of learning in the home, and into the relationship between families and educational practice, that raise new questions about the objectives, form and content of education in the past and today. This book was originally published as a special issue of the *Oxford Review of Education*.

Christina de Bellaigue is Associate Professor in Modern History at Exeter College, University of Oxford, UK. She is the author of *Educating women: schooling and identity in England and France, 1800–1867* (2007) and has published articles on the history of female education, comparative education, women and professionalization, and the history of reading. She is currently working on a comparative study of social mobility in nineteenth-century Britain and France, and on the history of the PNEU in the British Empire.

Home Education in Historical Perspective

Domestic pedagogies in England and Wales, 1750–1900

Edited by
Christina de Bellaigue

LONDON AND NEW YORK

First published 2016
by Routledge
2 Park Square, Milton Park, Abingdon, Oxon, OX14 4RN, UK

and by Routledge
711 Third Avenue, New York, NY 10017, USA

Routledge is an imprint of the Taylor & Francis Group, an informa business

© 2016 Taylor & Francis

All rights reserved. No part of this book may be reprinted or reproduced or utilised in any form or by any electronic, mechanical, or other means, now known or hereafter invented, including photocopying and recording, or in any information storage or retrieval system, without permission in writing from the publishers.

Trademark notice: Product or corporate names may be trademarks or registered trademarks, and are used only for identification and explanation without intent to infringe.

British Library Cataloguing in Publication Data
A catalogue record for this book is available from the British Library

ISBN13: 978-1-138-64389-5

Typeset in Plantin
by diacriTech, Chennai

Publisher's Note
The publisher accepts responsibility for any inconsistencies that may have arisen during the conversion of this book from journal articles to book chapters, namely the possible inclusion of journal terminology.

Disclaimer
Every effort has been made to contact copyright holders for their permission to reprint material in this book. The publishers would be grateful to hear from any copyright holder who is not here acknowledged and will undertake to rectify any errors or omissions in future editions of this book.

Contents

Citation Information vii
Notes on Contributors ix

Introduction - Home education 1750–1900: domestic pedagogies
in England and Wales in historical perspective 1
Christina de Bellaigue

1. The home education of girls in the eighteenth-century novel:
   'the pernicious effects of an improper education' 10
   Katie Halsey

2. The pedagogy of conversation in the home: 'familiar conversation'
   as a pedagogical tool in eighteenth and nineteenth-century England 27
   Michèle Cohen

3. Children's literature, the home, and the debate on
   public versus private education, c.1760–1845 44
   M. O. Grenby

4. Education in the working-class home: modes of learning
   as revealed by nineteenth-century criminal records 62
   Rosalind Crone

5. Charlotte Mason, home education and the Parents' National
   Educational Union in the late nineteenth century 81
   Christina de Bellaigue

6. Self-education, class and gender in Edwardian Britain:
   women in lower middle class families 98
   Gillian Sutherland

CONTENTS

7. Home education: then and now   114
   Richard Davies

   Index   129

Citation Information

The chapters in this book were originally published in *Oxford Review of Education*, volume 41, issue 4 (August 2015). When citing this material, please use the original page numbering for each article, as follows:

Introduction
Home education 1750–1900: domestic pedagogies in England and Wales in historical perspective
Christina de Bellaigue
Oxford Review of Education, volume 41, issue 4 (August 2015), 421–429

Chapter 1
The home education of girls in the eighteenth-century novel: 'the pernicious effects of an improper education'
Katie Halsey
Oxford Review of Education, volume 41, issue 4 (August 2015), 430–446

Chapter 2
The pedagogy of conversation in the home: 'familiar conversation' as a pedagogical tool in eighteenth and nineteenth-century England
Michèle Cohen
Oxford Review of Education, volume 41, issue 4 (August 2015), 447–463

Chapter 3
Children's literature, the home, and the debate on public versus private education, c.1760–1845
M. O. Grenby
Oxford Review of Education, volume 41, issue 4 (August 2015), 464–481

Chapter 4
Education in the working-class home: modes of learning as revealed by nineteenth-century criminal records
Rosalind Crone
Oxford Review of Education, volume 41, issue 4 (August 2015), 482–500

CITATION INFORMATION

Chapter 5
Charlotte Mason, home education and the Parents' National Educational Union in the late nineteenth century
Christina de Bellaigue
Oxford Review of Education, volume 41, issue 4 (August 2015), 501–517

Chapter 6
Self-education, class and gender in Edwardian Britain: women in lower middle class families
Gillian Sutherland
Oxford Review of Education, volume 41, issue 4 (August 2015), 518–533

Chapter 7
Home education: then and now
Richard Davies
Oxford Review of Education, volume 41, issue 4 (August 2015), 534–548

For any permission-related enquiries please visit:
http://www.tandfonline.com/page/help/permissions

Notes on Contributors

Michèle Cohen is Emeritus Professor in Humanities at Richmond University in London, and Visiting Professor at UCL Institute of Education, University of London, UK. Her main research areas are education, language, gender and national character in the long eighteenth century, lately focusing on 'conversation' in relation to domestic education. Her publications include *Fashioning masculinity: National identities and language in the eighteenth century* (1996). She is working on a monograph on the cultural history of education in the long eighteenth century.

Rosalind Crone is Senior Lecturer in History at The Open University, UK, author of *Violent Victorians: Popular Entertainment in Nineteenth-Century London* (2012), editor of volume four of *The Making of the Modern Police, 1780–1914: Policing Entertainment* (2014), co-editor of several books on the history of reading, and has published a range of articles on popular culture, crime and literacy in nineteenth-century England. She is currently writing a monograph on prisoner education programmes in the nineteenth century.

Richard Davies is Lecturer in Education at Aberystwyth University, UK. His research interests are primarily in virtue ethics, and informal and alternative educational practices. His family home educate.

Christina de Bellaigue is Associate Professor in Modern History at Exeter College, Oxford, UK. She is the author of *Educating Women: Schooling and Identity in England and France, 1800–1867* (2007) and has published on female education, comparative education and the history of reading.

M. O. Grenby is Professor of Eighteenth-Century Studies in the School of English at Newcastle University, UK. He is the author of books on children's literature, eighteenth-century novels and pre-modern child readers.

Katie Halsey is Senior Lecturer in Eighteenth-Century Literature at the University of Stirling, UK. Her publications include *Jane Austen and her Readers,1787–1945* (2012), *The History of Reading* (with Rosalind Crone and Shafquat Towheed, 2011), *The History of Reading: Evidence from the British Isles, 1750–1950* (with W. R. Owens, 2011), and *The Concept and Practice of*

NOTES ON CONTRIBUTORS

Conversation in the Long Eighteenth Century (with Jane Slinn, 2008). Her research interests include eighteenth-century and Romantic-period novels, the history of reading, and print culture more broadly. She has published in all of these areas.

Gillian Sutherland is a Fellow of Newnham College, Cambridge, UK, where she served as Director of Studies in History, Gwatkin Lecturer and Vice-Principal. Now retired from full-time teaching, she continues to pursue her own research and writing. She has worked extensively on the social history and politics of education in nineteenth and twentieth-century Britain. Her most recent publications include *Faith, Duty and the Power of Mind: The Cloughs and their Circle 1820–1960* (2006) and, with Christopher Stray, 'Mass markets: education' in Vol. VI of *The Cambridge History of the Book in Britain* (2009). Her book, *In Search of the New Woman: Middle-Class Women and Work in Britain 1870–1914*, was published in February 2015. She is Chairman of Governors of the Stephen Perse Foundation.

INTRODUCTION

Home education 1750–1900: domestic pedagogies in England and Wales in historical perspective

Christina de Bellaigue

Exeter College, Oxford, UK

Since the seventeenth century a growing body of advice literature, educational treatises and policy has been encouraging parents to play an active part in the education and instruction of their children (Fletcher, 2008, pp. 37–52; Grant, 2013, pp. 115–119). The focus of historians of education, however, has been on institutional instruction and the role of government in education. Consequently, we still know relatively little about the history of education beyond the school walls, but new research on the history of the book, on Enlightenment educational philosophy, and on the history of parenthood, has revealed the significance of domestic instruction among middle and upper class families in the late eighteenth century (Bailey, 2012; Grenby, 2011; Hilton, Styles, & Watson, 1997; Hilton & Shefrin, 2009). At the same time, research on literacy has suggested the importance of home learning for the children of the working classes in the nineteenth century (Rose, 2002; Vincent, 1981). Current research also draws attention to the role of home and family in education, noting the impact that family culture can have on educational outcomes (Dearden, Sibieta, & Sylva, 2011; Hart & Risley, 1995). And, the number of children being educated primarily at home is growing, rising in the UK from about 20 families in 1977 to 80,000 families in 2009 (Badman, 2009).

This Special Issue builds on the new historical research, and responds to the contemporary interest in the educational work of home and family.[1] Its six historical papers enable a better understanding of the history of home education, both as a philosophy and as a practice. The contributors approach this history from a range of perspectives. They draw on evidence from fiction, from book history, from advice literature, from prison records, memoirs, letters and diaries, to offer studies which shed new light on home education in Britain from 1750 to 1900. They reveal shifts in conceptions of the educational function of the home over time, and uncover varying ways in which domestic pedagogical strategies have been implemented. In the process, these studies demonstrate the continuing importance of the education offered at home even as institutional provision was expanding in the nineteenth century. They also call into question a tendency to over-emphasise the distinction between learning in the home and institutional instruction. As the final paper by Richard Davies suggests, together these articles illuminate a history that suggests new ways to think about current concerns and practice.

This Introduction sets the historical papers in context, considers the ways in which home education might be defined and interpreted, and highlights commonalities which merit further historical investigation. In his concluding commentary, Davies approaches the historical case-studies from the perspective of a philosopher and contemporary practitioner of Elective Home Education (EHE). He draws out common themes more fully and raises issues of particular relevance to home education today.

Focusing on the period 1750–1900 offers insights into ideas of domestic instruction that were particularly influential and enduring. While the nineteenth century saw the gradual expansion of school provision in England and Wales, and the professionalisation of teaching, this process was slower and more complex than in France, Germany or the USA (Green, 1990; Muller, Ringer, & Simon, 1987; Sutherland, 1990). It was not until the Forster Act in 1870 that anything like a nation-wide system of elementary schooling was established. And yet, literacy rates were as high as 60% in 1833, well before then (Vincent, 1989, p. 54). Similarly, while there were efforts in the 1860s and 1870s to rationalise the distribution of secondary institutions, it was not until 1902 that secondary schooling was systematically provided and funded (Sutherland, 1990, p. 152). Such figures testify to the longevity of a vital educational culture that did not depend on formal schooling. Instead, differing ideas and practices of home education competed with, co-existed with and complemented institutional instruction throughout the period, making the history of home education in England and Wales a particularly fruitful subject to explore.

The late eighteenth century saw the proliferation of treatises advocating the education of children in the home and promoting the role of parents in instruction. From the 1760s, theorists influenced by Rousseau began to develop new progressive pedagogies which emphasised child-centred learning and questioned the value of what was taught in schools (Cohen, 2009; Woodley, 2009a). At the same time, the influence of new ideas of sociability, the perceived failings of contemporary schools, and later the development of a distinctively British middle class conception of the home as a source of virtue, gave rise to the view that domestic instruction was far preferable to education at school for both boys and girls (Cohen, 2004; Davidoff & Hall, 2002, pp. 149–197; Woodley, 2009a). The papers here by Michèle Cohen on the pedagogy of conversation in the late eighteenth century, by Matthew Grenby on children's literature in the home during 1750–1850, and by Katie Halsey on domestic instruction in Romantic fiction, all shed new light on this key moment, which prompted the development of pedagogical approaches that made a virtue of their domestic origins.

Such ideas and pedagogies were principally directed towards and consumed by the middle and upper classes, who had the luxury of choice in determining how their children should be educated. However, even as the virtues of private education were being trumpeted, some were acknowledging that institutional education might be necessary or even have advantages. Prominent novelists used their fictions to explore the wider implications of domestic education for the position of women in society, itself seen as an indicator of the health of the wider nation (Halsey, this issue). Arguments about the need for an education that would shape national character undermined those in favour of the individual and intimate approach promoted by home educators (Cohen, 2004, p. 19). A growing number of voices began to argue that school education was necessary—particularly for boys, who needed to leave the feminine domestic world and in order to achieve manly independence (Tosh, 1999, pp. 110–115). Changing conceptions of the place of women in society also called into question the appropriateness of home education for girls (Halsey, this issue). At the same time, shifting patterns of sociability, and new conceptions of the way knowledge should be shared, further devalorised domestic instruction (Cohen, this issue). The professionalisation of teaching and the specialisation of knowledge and research also had an impact (Bellaigue, 2001; Rothblatt, 1968, 1976).

By the middle of the nineteenth century, those arguing in favour of home education for the elite were a minority. At the same time, the perception that families of the middle and working classes were inadequate to the task of educating their children was prompting greater intervention by the state (Crone, this issue; Musgrove, 1959, pp. 175–176; Woodley, 2009b, pp. 119–147). The home was losing its legitimacy as a source of knowledge and instruction. Christina de Bellaigue's paper on the popular home educationist Charlotte Mason demonstrates, however, that even at the end of the century, in the context of patchy institutional provision, significant numbers were still receiving much of their education in the home. In the same period, parents and educationists continued to express interest in the ideas of the late eighteenth-century theorists who had first argued in favour of domestic instruction, prompting some elite parents to seek alternatives to the dominant public school model of schooling.

For many families lower down the social scale, however, the question of choice was moot. Papers here by Rosalind Crone on modes of learning in the working class home in the nineteenth century, and by Gillian Sutherland, on self-education in the lower middle class at the turn of the nineteenth century, suggest that those with fewer resources needed to make the most of what was available. From the 1780s, growing numbers of working class children were attending privately-established working class schools and the institutions established by religious organisations. By 1850, there were two million children attending Sunday schools (Gardner, 1984; Laqueur, 1976, p. 44). Whatever arguments might be made in favour of domestic education, such numbers suggest that working class families were keen to use schools where they were available; and evidence from prison records suggests that those whose literate skills were most developed had usually acquired them in schools (Crone, this issue). By the late nineteenth century, mass schooling was established and, as Sutherland notes, 'it became increasingly difficult to find many who had had no encounter at all with formal provision' (Sutherland, this issue). However, this did not preclude educational activities in the home. Instead, Crone's work suggests that the home was becoming more, rather than less, important in the provision of occupational instruction. Similarly, the late nineteenth century saw large-scale engagement in efforts for self-improvement of the kind explored by Sutherland. By 1906, there were 13,052 members of the National Home Reading Union (Snape, 2002, p. 103). While such movements might not have conformed to the ideals of late eighteenth-century educational theorists, they demonstrate the continuing use of the home as an educational space even as professional educators were asserting the importance of trained teachers and specialised sites for instruction.

As this rapid overview intimates, the definition of what constituted home education changed over the period. Even today, as Richard Davies notes, it is a difficult term to define (Davies, this issue). It functions as an umbrella phrase covering a very broad range of practices, from the politically charged notion of 'home-schooling'— which does not necessarily imply abstention from scholastic routines, that is most common among certain religious communities in the USA—to the commitment to autonomous learning implied by the notion of 'unschooling' and which has a counter-cultural connotation (Davies, this issue; Kunzman & Gaither, 2013, pp. 9–11). M. Gioria argues that attempts to define home education are counter-productive since 'there are as many reasons to educate at home as there are families who opt to do it' and notes that such definitional efforts imply a normative conception of education as schooling (quoted in Rothermel, 2011, p. 2009).[2] This conception, as the papers here reveal, is one that is historically specific and contingent. Indeed it was over the course of the period 1750–1900 that 'education' came to be seen as synonymous with 'schooling': that is with formal, specialised instruction in an institutional setting.

The contributors to this Special Issue have interpreted the term 'home education' broadly, partly in order to help uncover the historical process by which school education became established as the norm. The different papers thus reflect the diverse meanings of home education in the past as in the present, and also highlight the multiplicity of educational activities which took place in the home in the period 1750–1900. Paying attention to the specificity of terms used in different periods can be revealing. In the late eighteenth century, when an educational philosophy of home education was most clearly articulated, the term most commonly used was 'private education', meaning education conducted in the privacy of the home, rather than 'in public' at school. This was a value-laden phrase. Privacy then connoted domesticity, virtue, and a moral and serious approach to instruction and knowledge, in opposition to education in public, which connoted worldliness and superficiality, both of knowledge and of character. In the nineteenth century, the term 'home education' was more often used, and specifically deployed in contrast to 'school education', but the same period saw the emergence of the language of 'self-improvement' and 'self-education', terms which gave rise to many publications directed at the working class and lower middle class learners studied by Crone and Sutherland (Vincent, 1981, Part III). By the end of the nineteenth century, 'home education' was being deployed in multiple ways: simply to indicate that which was learned at home, more specifically to refer to the training of character and mind carried out in the home by parents, and also as a way to refer to the instruction of children in the 'home school-room'. What constituted 'home education' shifted continuously and varied according to context.

The boundaries and characteristics of 'home' were also mutable throughout the period; there might be little difference between the way children were taught at school and the way they were taught at home. Cohen and Bellaigue note that boys and girls taught at home might be subject to daily regimes and routines that echoed those adopted in schools. Similarly, schools might seek to model themselves on the home—this was particularly common in girls' schools, but the domestic character of English boys' schools was also something which struck foreign visitors. Even as schools expanded in the nineteenth century, efforts were made to preserve the perceived benefits of home education (Bellaigue, 2004, 2007). Grenby reveals the ways in which children's literature was produced for a market where the lines between home and school education were blurred, and the same texts might be considered appropriate for both (Grenby, this issue).

At the same time, the context in which the late eighteenth-century child received instruction at home might be very different to what twenty-first-century conceptions of home and family might imply. Grenby shows that William Godwin's children were incorporated into a rich multi-generational educational enterprise, which challenges modern conceptions of the distinction between public and private (Grenby, this issue). Moreover the boundary between home and school might be very porous, with parents seeking to shape the character of the education their children were offered at school (Grenby, this issue).

Examining ideas and practices of home education in the past, then, reveals that instruction offered from the home was not always viewed in opposition to that offered in schools. Rather, education at home often formed part of the varied education of children of all classes before mass and compulsory schooling was established. The historical analysis also underlines the ways in which scholastic and home instruction might interact, and calls into question any simple distinctions between home/domestic and institutional education in the past and today. As Sutherland and Davies suggest, rather than seeking to set up dichotomies between home and school and between formal and informal education, it may be more fruitful to think in terms of the individuals experiencing a range of educational environments and influences along a spectrum of formal to informal and which might blur the boundaries between home and school, rather than any singular 'education'. This re-conceptualisation of the range of educational experience might even help to break down the opposition between parental and professional conceptions of knowledge which dates back to the nineteenth century, and which continues to have damaging effects (Crozier, 1999).

HOME EDUCATION IN HISTORICAL PERSPECTIVE

The six historical papers also raise four key issues which need further study. The first concerns the extent to which the meaning and practice of home education has shifted with changing practices of family life and with demographic change. In the late eighteenth century, the importance of conversation to sociability, and the large size of elite households promoted a particular version of home education that emphasised intergenerational exchange, and friendship within the family (Cohen, this issue; Grenby, this issue). By the late nineteenth century, smaller family sizes, the ritualisation of family life, and the greater age-segregation of middle class homes—where children more often occupied specialised spaces apart from their parents and other adults—gave home education a different character (Gillis, 1996; Hamlett, 2010, pp. 112–114). The ways in which demography and the changing functions and practices of family life have shaped pedagogical practice in the home, and indeed outside the home, require deeper investigation.

The second issue concerns the question of agency in education. Both the architects of the familiar format studied by Cohen, and Charlotte Mason and her supporters, drew on Enlightenment theory to support the idea that children should have agency in their own learning. Crone and Sutherland highlight the ways in which, far from being the passive recipients of publicly-funded schooling, working class and lower middle class families developed complex educational strategies to make the most of the opportunities available to them, retaining some control over their educational trajectories. As Davies notes, to the extent that contemporary EHE practitioners share an educational outlook, it is that they all support some degree of autonomous learning by children—again this could be considered a question of protecting agency. More work is needed to track the intellectual history of this tradition and to consider the ways in which those espousing home education have contributed to pedagogical traditions seeking to privilege the agency of the individual in their own learning.

The third issue concerns gender and power. Throughout the period, it was principally mothers who took charge of the education of their children in the home. Cohen, Grenby and Bellaigue all reveal the seriousness with which many middle and upper class women undertook this task from the late eighteenth to the late nineteenth centuries, and the significant educational role of mothers has been demonstrated in several other studies (Crone, this issue; Humphries, 2010, p. 320; Shefrin, 2006). In the nineteenth century, the maternal responsibility for instruction gave women considerable cultural power in this period, giving rise to a female tradition of public moralism (Dabby, forthcoming; Hilton, 2007). One reason for the popularity of the PNEU was the way in which it conferred authority on mothers and legitimised their intellectual activity (Bellaigue, this issue). However, this division of labour also shored up traditional gender hierarchies, and the extent to which home education can be 'a means of domesticating not children, but mothers' is a subject which continues to be controversial in contemporary home education research (Davies, this issue; Kunzman & Gaither, 2013, pp. 14–15). At the same time, there were gendered dimensions to educational theory and practice, and it is clear that more girls than boys were being educated at home for the whole of this period. The idea that women were best educated at home in preparation for domestic life had traction far longer than any idea that gentleman might best be taught at home, and it still influenced the curriculum and careers' guidance for girls into the twentieth century. Further analysis of the complex relationship between gender and home education is needed.

One final issue raised by the historical analysis is the narrowness of contemporary conceptions of education. As Crone notes, the domestic curriculum could be usefully defined to include 'learning to crawl or speak, developing an awareness and later knowledge of identity and community, and cultivating and expanding the imaginative faculties' (Crone, this issue; Vincent, 1997). Similarly, home education might be defined to include occupational training as well as more canonical learning. Sutherland's paper highlights the myriad ways in which, beyond the school, lower middle class women sought to expand their educational horizons, drawing on multiple resources—chapel meetings, public libraries etc.—in their efforts. And Charlotte Mason's conception of the educational work done by parents was broad, incorporating the training of habit and character, nutritional choices, physical education, as well as more conventional educational activities. These expansive definitions undermine the notion of education as synonymous with schooling and propose a more flexible and inclusive conception of instruction and learning. They support a sense of education as a much larger and lengthier project, ranging over a much wider gamut of activities and experiences. They also suggest ways in which we could begin to expand understandings of education today, and to recognise more fully and appreciate the educational work done by agencies beyond the school, and by parents of all classes and cultures.

Notes

1. The papers in this Special Issue were presented at a workshop held in Oxford in June 2014 that was generously supported by the Oxford Modern European History Research Centre and by The Exeter College Fellows' Research Fund, Oxford. Exeter College also funded editorial assistance from Charlotte Bennett, to whom I owe many thanks. Her intellectual engagement with the project, and help in managing the editorial process, were invaluable. I would like to thank all the readers who kindly gave of their time and expertise in reviewing the papers here and am very grateful to Vicki Lloyd, Editorial Assistant of the ORE, and to John Furlong, Editor, for all their advice and support.
2. In this context, it is significant that one of the chief organs of home educators in the UK is 'Education Otherwise', which takes its name from a phrase in the 1944 Education Act. Similarly, an important new journal in the field is *Other Education: The Journal of Educational Alternatives*.

References

Badman, G. (2009). *Review into Elective Home Education in England*. London: TSO.
Bailey, J. (2012). *Parenting in England 1760–1830: Emotion, identity and generation*. Oxford: Oxford University Press.

Bellaigue, C. de (2001). The development of teaching as a profession for women before 1870. *Historical Journal, 44*, 963–988.

Bellaigue, C. de (2004). 'Educational homes' and 'Barrack-like schools': Cross-channel perspectives on secondary education for boys in mid-nineteenth century England and France. In D. Phillips & K. Ochs (Eds.), *Educational policy borrowing: Historical perspectives*, [Special issue] Oxford Studies in Comparative Education, *14*(2), 89–108.

Bellaigue, C. de (2007). *Educating women: Schooling and identity in England and France, 1800–1867*. Oxford: Oxford University Press.

Cohen, M. (2004). Gender and the private/public debate on education in the long eighteenth century. In R. Aldrich (Ed.), *Public or private education. Lessons from history*, (pp. 16–35). London: Routledge.

Cohen, M. (2009). Familiar conversation: The role of the 'familiar format' in education in 18th and 19thC England. In M. Hilton & J. Shefrin (Eds.), *Educating the child in enlightenment Britain. Beliefs, cultures, practices* (pp. 99–116). Farnham: Ashgate.

Crozier, G. (1999). Is it a case of 'We know when we're not wanted?' The parents' perspective on parent–teacher roles and relationships. *Educational Research, 41*, 315–328.

Dabby, B. (forthcoming). *Women as public moralists: From the Bluestockings to Virginia Woolf*. London: Royal Historical Society—Studies in History.

Davidoff, L., & Hall, C. (2002). *Family fortunes: Men and women of the English middle class 1780–1850*. London: Routledge.

Dearden, L., Sibieta, L., & Sylva, K. (2011). The socioeconomic gradient in early child outcomes: Evidence from the Millenium Cohort Study. *Longitudinal and Life Courses Studies, 2*, 19–40.

Fletcher, A. (2008). *Growing up in England. The experience of childhood, 1600–1914*. London & New Haven, CT: Yale University Press.

Gardner, P. (1984). *The lost elementary schools of Victorian England*. London: Croom Helm.

Gillis, J. (1996). Making time for family: The invention of family time(s) and the reinvention of family history. *Journal of Family History, 21*(4), 4–21.

Grant, J. (2013). Parent–child relations in Western Europe and North America, 1500–present. In P. Fass (Ed.), *Childhood in the Western world* (pp. 103–124). London: Routledge.

Green, A. (1990). *Education and state formation: The rise of education systems in England, France and the USA*. New York: St Martin's Press.

Grenby, M. O. (2011). *The child reader, 1700–1840*. Cambridge: Cambridge University Press.

Hamlett, J. (2010). *Material relations: Domestic interiors and middle class families in England, 1850–1910*. Manchester: Manchester University Press.

Hart, B., & Risley, T. R. (1995). *Meaningful differences in the every day experiences of young American children*. Baltimore, MD: Brookes.

Hilton, M. (2007). *Women and the shaping of the nation's young: Education and public doctrine in Britain 1750–1850*. Farnham: Ashgate.

Hilton, M., & Shefrin, J. (2009). Introduction. In M. Hilton & J. Shefrin (Eds.), *Educating the child in Enlightenment Britain. Beliefs, cultures, practices* (pp. 1–20). Farnham: Ashgate.

Hilton, M., Styles, M., & Watson, V. (Eds.). (1997). *Opening the nursery door. Reading, writing and childhood 1600–1900* (pp. 1–13). London: Routledge.

Humphries, J. (2010). *Childhood and child labour in the British industrial revolution*. Cambridge: Cambridge University Press.

Kunzman, R., & Gaither, M. (2013). Homeschooling: A comprehensive survey of the literature. *Other Education: The Journal of Educational Alternatives, 2*, 4–59.

Laqueur, T. W. (1976). *Religion and respectability, Sunday schools and working class culture 1780–1850*. London & New Haven, CT: Yale University Press.

Muller, D., Ringer, F., & Simon, B. (1987). *The rise of the modern educational system. Structural change and social reproduction, 1870–1920*. Cambridge: Cambridge University Press.

Musgrove, F. (1959). Middle class families and schools, 1780–1880: Interaction and exchange of function between institutions. *Sociological Review, 7*(12), 169–178.

Rose, J. (2002). *The intellectual life of the British working classes.* London & New Haven, CT: Yale Nota Bene.

Rothblatt, S. (1968). *The revolution of the dons.* Cambridge: Cambridge University Press.

Rothblatt, S. (1976). *Tradition and change in English liberal education.* London: Faber & Faber.

Rothermel, P. (2011). Setting the record straight: Interviews with a hundred British home educating families. *Journal of Unschooling and Alternative Learning, 5*(10), 20–57.

Shefrin, J. (2006). Governesses to their children. Royal and aristocratic mothers educating daughters in the reign of George III. In A. Immel & M. Witmore (Eds.), *Childhood and children's books in early modern Europe, 1550–1800.* (pp. 181–212). Milton Park: Routledge.

Snape, R. (2002). The National Home Reading Union. *Journal of Victorian Culture, 7,* 86–110.

Sutherland, G. (1990). Education. In F. M. L. Thompson (Ed.), *Cambridge social history, vol. III* (pp. 119–171). Cambridge: Cambridge University Press.

Tosh, J. (1999). *A man's place. Masculinity and the middle class home in Victorian England.* London & New Haven, CT: Yale University Press.

Vincent, D. (1981). *Bread knowledge and freedom. A study of nineteenth century working class autobiography.* London: Europa.

Vincent, D. (1989). *Literacy and popular culture, 1780–1914.* Cambridge: Cambridge University Press.

Vincent, D. (1997). The domestic and the official curriculum in 19thC England. In M. Hilton, M. Styles, & V. Watson (Eds.), *Opening the nursery door. Reading, writing and childhood 1600–1900* (pp. 161–179). London: Routledge.

Woodley, S. (2009a). 'Oh miserable and most ruinous measure': The debate between private and public education in Britain, 1760–1800. In M. Hilton & J. Shefrin (Eds.), *Educating the child in Enlightenment Britain. Beliefs, cultures, practices* (pp. 21–40). Farnham: Ashgate.

Woodley, S. (2009b). *'Go to school they shall not': Home education and the middle classes in Britain 1760–1900* (DPhil dissertation). Oxford.

The home education of girls in the eighteenth-century novel: 'the pernicious effects of an improper education'

Katie Halsey
University of Stirling, UK

This essay explores the relationship between theories of domestic pedagogy as articulated in eighteenth-century conduct books, and fictional representations of home education in novels of the period. The fictional discussions of domestic pedagogy interrogate eighteenth-century assumptions about the innate superiority of a domestic education for women. In so doing, they participate in a much wider eighteenth-century and Regency-period debate about the proper role of women in public life. In order to make the argument that a woman's education was vital to the public welfare of the nation, writers from Mary Wollstonecraft to Jane Austen shifted the grounds of the debate, making the previously private into a matter of public concern. Early eighteenth-century ideals of domestic education, which kept women firmly in the private sphere, therefore began to seem outdated.

Scenes of domestic education are ubiquitous in novels of all kinds in the eighteenth and early nineteenth centuries. From the hotly politicised fiction of William Godwin to the domestic novels of Jane Austen, discussions of education frequently form the backdrop, and sometimes the central action, of novels of the period. In the last pages of Elizabeth Inchbald's *A Simple Story* (1791), for example, her readers are explicitly asked to judge between 'the pernicious effects of an improper education' and the likely results of 'A PROPER EDUCATION' (Inchbald, 1967 [1791], pp. 337–338). The generic fluidity of the early novel gave novelists the opportunity to recast philosophical and educational theory into fictional form, and allowed them to enter into the era's great cultural debates about the nature, purpose and role of education in the life of the individual and of the nation. As Sophia

HOME EDUCATION IN HISTORICAL PERSPECTIVE

Woodley argues, the eighteenth-century debate over whether a public or private education was superior 'served as a site where major philosophical and political issues of the day could be contested' (Woodley, 2009, p. 21). Fiction writers of both sexes, and of all political, religious and class affiliations, wished to have their say, and they did so in many and various ways.

In this essay, I consider a survey of depictions of education in eighteenth-century and Regency novels, with a particular focus on the 1790s, arguing throughout that these representations should be read as part of a much wider debate about the role of women in the public life of the nation. Comparing these fictional representations to the theory articulated in a survey of some 40 eighteenth-century conduct books and works of educational theory (see References section for a full list of works consulted), I shall argue that the contradictions and ambivalence that characterise discussions of domestic education represent and indeed sometimes epitomise ambivalent attitudes towards the increasing fluidity of the boundaries between private and public spheres in the eighteenth century. My choice of texts deliberately includes writers from the beginning of the 'long' eighteenth century to the end of the Regency period (covering the period 1660–1830), and takes account of writers from across the political spectrum, and the gamut of religious affiliations, to provide as wide a survey as possible. As Michèle Cohen points out, 'the history of education is central to an understanding of the positioning of males and females as gendered beings since the Enlightenment' (Cohen, 2004, p. 15). It is equally true that an understanding of eighteenth-century anxieties over gender roles is central to an understanding of the history of education.

Much educational theory of the eighteenth century and Regency periods appears in conduct books, particularly conduct books written for women. These works engage strongly with the educational theories propounded by Locke and Rousseau, and they attempt to educate readers into virtue. Conduct books, as Nancy Armstrong rightly points out, 'presented—in actuality, still present—readers with ideology in its most powerful form' (Armstrong, 1987, p. 97). A careful examination of the conduct literature written for women of the eighteenth and early-nineteenth centuries therefore reminds us of the matters of pressing concern to eighteenth-century and Romantic-period readers and writers. Conduct books, as Barbara Zaczek suggests, 'attempt to solve the conflict between a real life and an ideal', being 'designed to replace the existing set of values with a new one and turn the reality into the desired model' (Zaczek, 1997, p. 29), and hence their discussions about education can helpfully identify for us both existing values, and various attempts to solve perceived problems. The debates most commonly canvassed in conduct literature are as follows: the relative value of a public or private education; the dubious value of ornamental 'accomplishments'; the role and purpose of reading; the dangers of excessive emotion or 'feeling'; 'free-thinking' *versus* religious authority; the role of reason in religion; how to inculcate moral principles; the perils and charms of the fashionable life; and, more broadly, the proper occupations for women.

It is clear that many writers of conduct literature were participating in a vigorous and often heartfelt debate about female education, the outcome of which, they believed, would affect the very future of the nation. As early as 1695, Mary Astell proposed a proper Christian education as the best way to combat 'the degeneracy of the present Age' (Astell, 1695, p. 110). Nearly 100 years later, Mary Wollstonecraft's proposed 'revolution in female manners', had the same impetus, being based on the idea that women should 'labour by reforming themselves, to reform the world' (Wollstonecraft, 1992 [1792], p. 113). The publication of Rousseau's *Emile* in 1762 prompted a large number of women to write books on girls' education which drew on their own experience of educating children in the home to counter Rousseau's narrative of Sophie's education (Rousseau, 1913 [1762]). And, as Rebecca Davies argues, appeals to this specifically maternal authority allowed such women into the public sphere as professional writers, thus complicating the gender ideologies that the books seem to endorse (Davies, 2014).

It is a truism in most of the conduct literature of the early part of the century that girls should be educated in the home, under the careful supervision of parents as well as governesses (Mary Astell (1695) and Bathsua Makin (2002 [1673]) do favour female schools in the late seventeenth century, but they are unusual in so doing). As Davies points out, it was an 'eighteenth-century expectation that mothers foster intellectual growth in children' (Davies, 2014, p. 1). This attitude is based on an assumption that seclusion from the world will guarantee a more virtuous character, and that mothers are the most appropriate educators of children because they will supervise their moral, religious and social education most carefully. This view is articulated most clearly in Vicesimus Knox's *Liberal Education* (1781). Indeed, much early eighteenth-century advice literature simply takes for granted that the class of young women who will be educated at all will be educated at home. In John Essex's *The Ladies Conduct; or, Rules for Education* of 1722, for example, Essex compares the education of girls favourably to that of boys, suggesting that 'much is owing to the Pride and Stubbornness of [boys'] Tempers; many Faults in their School Education; and their too early going Abroad into the World', while 'the training up of Daughters is more agreeable and easy', because it happens at home (Essex, 1722, p. 2). Alexander Monro's *The Professor's Daughter. An Essay on Female Conduct* (1739–1745) lays out the content of such an education:

> Girls of your Station are generally taught Reading, Writing, Arithmetick, Dancing, Musick, S[e]wing with all the other Parts of what is called Women's work, Dressing, Repetitions of some pious Performances, and then generally without being desired you study Poems Plays Novels and Romances. To these I wou'd add some Languages besides that of the Country Mercating [marketing], Book keeping, Designing, Geography, History, Good Manners, natural Religion, reveal'd Religion. (Monro, 1996, p. 9)

Those writers who wished to define and promote virtuous female conduct assumed that mothers (and, to a far lesser degree, fathers), assisted by governesses and visiting masters, would take responsibility for the education of their daughters, and that education would take place as conversations, or lessons, in the home. As late as 1787, John Bennett could suggest that the 'famous question about a public or private education' had never been raised in relation to girls, although it had of course dominated discourse about boys' education for several years by then (Bennett, 1787, p. 138). An anti-schools prejudice was common well into the 1790s and beyond—Thomas Gisborne prefers 'the domestic plan of education for the female sex' on the grounds that it is impossible to guard against 'the pernicious society of those who are not so well principled as themselves' at a boarding school, and that emulation of her peers may lead a girl into the sins of envy and avarice (Gisborne, 1996 [1797], p. 57). Characteristically oppositional, Mary Wollstonecraft set herself against the prevailing assumption of the superiority of a domestic education, when she writes that 'I do not believe that a private education can work the wonders which some sanguine writers have attributed to it' (Wollstonecraft, 1992 [1792], p. 86). Figure 1 demonstrates the perception that schools might even lead girls into the path of sexual ruin, while in Figure 2 we see an idealised version of the domestic education that functions as the explicit and implicit opposite of the criticisms of schools, where a mother fondly instructs her own child.

Schools for young women are stigmatised as promoting exterior 'accomplishments' or 'acquirements' (singing, dancing, playing the piano, speaking Italian) at the expense of internal virtue, and criticised for their emphasis on external manners, rather than internal spiritual growth. John Bennett notes austerely that '[t]he education of women is unfortunately directed rather to such accomplishments, as will enable them to make a noise and sparkle in the world, than to those qualities, which might insure their comfort here, and happiness hereafter' (Bennett, 1789, vol. 1, p. 6), while Hannah More bemoans the way 'our daughters' are educated 'for the transient period of youth', asking, 'Do we not educate them for a crowd, forgetting that they are to live at home? for the world, and not for themselves? for show, and not for use?' (More, 1801 [1799], vol. 1, p. 72). Hester Chapone tells her young (fictional) correspondent that the 'chief of her accomplishments' will be 'a competent share of reading, well-chosen and properly regulated', and that her 'chief delight' will be in 'those persons and those books from which you can learn true wisdom' (Chapone, 1996 [1773], pp. 187, 6). Indeed, the writers of conduct books, whatever their political and religious motivation, unite against both schools and 'accomplishments' to an extent that suggests they are being used as the scapegoats for something else: perhaps an indeterminate sense that female display of any kind could pose a challenge to accepted norms of female behaviour. Both the explicit criticisms of schools in conduct books, and the criticisms of 'accomplishments' are therefore part of the same broader debate: that of the place of women in the public sphere. In privileging the domestic over the world, private over public, internal over external, these writers reveal pressing eighteenth-century anxieties about the ways in which women—including the very women who wrote educational manuals—were beginning to transgress the boundaries between the private and public spheres.

Thus the vigour of the debate surrounding female education was at least partly generated by uncertainty and fears over changing norms and standards of female behaviour. By the late eighteenth century, two Jacobite revolutions (of 1715 and 1745) and the American War of Independence had shaken up the British governing

Figure 1. *A Boarding School Miss taking an Evening Lesson!!* (1831) Lewis Walpole Library MS 831.00.00.34+. Courtesy of The Lewis Walpole Library, Yale University

classes, and in the unsettled years before and immediately after the French Revolution, revolutionary radical ideas demanded the serious attention, not only of politicians and intellectuals, but of many women of the literate classes. Family dynamics were changing; literacy (and particularly female literacy) was rising, middle class women had more leisure than ever before, and new ideas could be disseminated

HOME EDUCATION IN HISTORICAL PERSPECTIVE

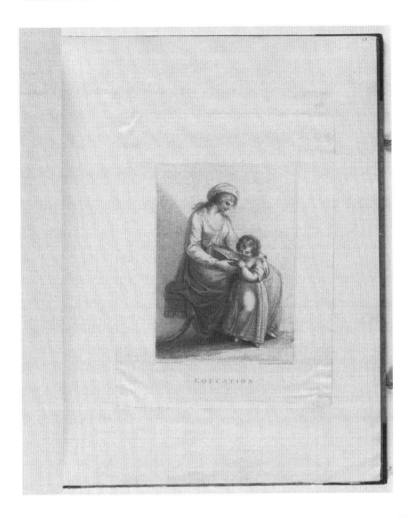

Figure 2. *Education* Lewis Walpole Library, MS 49 3588 v. 2 Folio. Courtesy of The Lewis Walpole Library, Yale University

through the newspapers, periodical press and circulating libraries.[1] Politically radical writers had the opportunity of reaching a literate female audience, and politically conservative writers faced the challenges of refuting a tide of radical and revolutionary ideas. Linda Colley and others have suggested that an ideology of separate sexual spheres was being 'increasingly prescribed in theory, yet increasingly broken through in practice', in the half century after the American war (Colley, 1992, p. 250). Conservative moralists thus perceived the domestic ideal as under threat, not just from revolutionary ideas, but from the common practice of the nation's wives and mothers. While Mary Wollstonecraft and the circle around her future husband William Godwin posited a new version of femininity based on the idea that women, like men, are primarily rational creatures, conservative writers felt the need to reiterate their vision of femininity, stressing that men and women are fundamentally different, and thus that the rules that govern the conduct of women should be different to those that apply to men. Whereas men should 'plunge into business' (Gregory, 1795 [1761], p. 21), for example, '[d]omestic qualifications' are 'confessedly the highest point of usefulness' in the female sex (Bennett, 1789, vol. 1, p. 6). Given that claims of maternal authority based on their role as domestic educators had given women a voice in the public sphere of print culture, it is perhaps not surprising that debates over gender roles so frequently appear as scenes of domestic education in the novels of the period.

The stereotypes about the shallowness and pernicious nature of boarding-school education, and hence the superiority of its opposite—a domestic education—represented in Figures 1 and 2 appear equally frequently in novels. In Inchbald's *A Simple Story*, for example, we hear that the heroine Miss Milner was

> consigned [...] to a Protestant boarding-school, from whence she was sent with merely such sentiments of religion, as young ladies of fashion mostly imbibe. Her little heart employed in all the endless pursuits of personal accomplishment had left her mind without one ornament, except those which nature gave, and even they were not wholly preserved from the ravages made by its rival, *Art*. (Inchbald, 1967 [1791], pp. 4–5)

The 'merely' and 'mostly' in this brief extract clearly reveal common perceptions of fashionable boarding schools in the 1790s, as well as Inchbald's own pro-Catholic agenda. In Mary Hays's *Memoirs of Emma Courtney* (1796), the heroine finds herself miserable at her boarding school, 'consigned, with my companions, to ignorant, splenetic, teachers, who encouraged not my emulations, and who sported with the acuteness of my sensations' (Hays, 1996 [1796], p. 16). The focus in both texts is on the 'ignorance' encountered in boarding establishments, as well as the harm done to impressionable young women by such ignorance. In Jane Austen's *Emma* (1815), Austen tells her readers a great deal about the reputation of most boarding schools through her description of Mrs Goddard's school:

> Mrs. Goddard was the mistress of a School—not of a seminary, or an establishment, or any thing which professed, in long sentences of refined nonsense, to combine liberal acquirements with elegant morality upon new principles and new systems—and where young ladies for enormous pay might be screwed out of health and into vanity—but a real, honest, old-fashioned Boarding-school, where a reasonable quantity of accomplishments were sold at a reasonable price, and where girls might be sent to be out of the way and scramble themselves into a little education, without any danger of coming back prodigies. Mrs. Goddard's school was in high repute—and very deservedly; for Highbury was reckoned a particularly healthy spot: she had an ample house and garden, gave the children plenty of wholesome food, let them run about a great deal in the summer, and in winter dressed their chilblains with her own hands. It was no wonder that a train of twenty young couple now walked after her to church. (Austen, 2005 [1815], p. 21)

Unlike the fashionable 'seminaries' or 'establishments' depicted in Figure 1, Mrs Goddard's school is one where children remain healthy, and do not learn decorative accomplishments at the expense of real lessons. Nonetheless, Austen's depiction of even a 'real, honest, old-fashioned Boarding-school' is not entirely positive, since the children must merely 'scramble themselves into' an education, and have no guarantee that they will actually learn anything that will be of use to them in their lives. Again, ignorance is foregrounded, and the commercial imperatives that prioritised financial profit at the expense of real education are revealed. These criticisms of schools suggest that a prevailing belief in the value of domestic education still continued, well into the Regency period.

As in the conduct literature, the disapproval of 'accomplishments' is ubiquitous in fiction of the long eighteenth century, and is nicely illustrated by this conversation from Eliza Haywood's *The History of Miss Betsy Thoughtless* (1751). Mr Goodman, Betsy's guardian, commends Betsy to Alderman Saving as a daughter-in-law, saying that Betsy is 'of a good family, had a very pretty fortune of her own, and suitable accomplishments'. Saving replies:

> … A good family! Very pleasant i'faith. Will a good family go to market?—will it buy a joint of mutton at the butcher's?—Or a pretty gown at the mercer's? Then, a pretty fortune you say;—enough it may be to squander away at cards and masquerades, for a month or two. She has suitable accomplishments too;—yes, indeed, they are suitable ones, I believe:—I suppose she can sing, dance, and jabber a little French; but I'll be hanged if she knows how to make a pye, or a pudding, or to teach her maid to do it. (Haywood, 1997 [1751], p. 32)

Alderman Saving is, of course, a caricature, but his comments echo many others, made by more admirable characters in other novels, and, indeed, even chime with Austen's comments about Miss Goddard's school. His comments reflect his belief that a woman's proper role is to manage her household economically and effectively, and also reveal his dislike of women's increasing involvement in the public sphere. Such sentiments were not unusual.

It might therefore appear that novelists wholeheartedly endorse the same kinds of attitudes that we have seen in conduct books. But novels also problematise the idea that a domestic education is necessarily better for girls. In Daniel Defoe's *Moll Flanders* (1722), the titular heroine receives an exemplary domestic education for a working-class woman, learning to be 'housewifely and clean', to be an excellent needlewoman, and to be 'very mannerly, and with good behaviour' (Defoe, 2004 [1722], p. 15). Indeed, when she is adopted into a gentry-class family, the narrator tells us that she receives 'all the advantages' of a gentlewoman's education, learning to dance, to speak French, to write, to sing and to play the harpsichord (p. 18). But Moll's education, instead of arming her with virtue and thus strengthening her against the various temptations of the world, makes her vain, and hence sows the seeds of her almost-immediate seduction by the elder son of the family, and her subsequent career of prostitution and theft. We can read this as a class-based criticism; there is indeed a strong sense that in raising Moll above her original milieu, in which she is industrious and honest, the gentlewoman who adopts her also ruins her. But we could also see this as reflecting a broader ambivalence about the benefits of educating women at home. Although commentators of the early eighteenth century almost universally agree that the family circle was the only safe place for a woman to receive her education, keeping her safe from the contagions of school,

Moll's story suggests that, in fact, even the domestic hearth and home may be rendered unsafe by education.

While, as in Betsy Thoughtless's case, fashionable accomplishments are very often considered to be the preserve of boarding schools, this is not always so, as we will see in the discussion of Jane Austen's *Mansfield Park* (1814). And, by the end of the eighteenth century, although stereotypes of boarding schools were still frequently used as a shorthand for a facile and worthless education, writers of fiction were also beginning to question the unthinking assumption that a domestic education necessarily equipped a girl well for life in the wider world. Frances Burney's *Evelina* (1778) deals almost entirely with this theme—Evelina's innate goodness keeps her safe in the world as she enters it, but she is frequently disconcerted, discomforted and even hurt by her failures to understand the customs and practices of polite society. As her guardian Mr Villars himself notes, although he himself was the one who decided that she should receive a rural education and be kept strictly from the metropolitan world, 'Alas, my child, the artlessness of your nature, and the simplicity of your education, alike unfit you for the thorny paths of the great and busy world …' (Burney, 2000 [1778], p. 223). It is clear that secluded retirement from the world, however excellent the education one may receive there may be, is a poor preparation for the real world of the eighteenth-century marriage market. Writers of fiction are thus pointing out the potential inconsistencies in the advice literature, which recommends that daughters should be kept entirely safe within the domestic sphere from any potentially corrupting influence, because an education which maintains their innocence and purity will make them more marriageable. As the fiction demonstrates, in fact the very innocence and purity that makes them attractive also makes them more vulnerable to rakes, fortune-hunters and unscrupulous men of all kinds.

Charlotte Lennox's *Female Quixote* (1752) makes the point about the dangers of rural seclusion through a different set of examples from Burney's. Its heroine, Arabella, has an excessive fondness for the romances that she finds in her reclusive father's library. Because she is never exposed to any countermanding influences, she takes these romances entirely seriously and literally, with very comical effects. 'Her Ideas, from the Manner of her Life, and the Objects around her, had taken a romantic Turn; and, supposing Romances were real Pictures of Life, from them she drew all her Notions and Expectations' (Lennox, 2008 [1752], p. 7). After a series of increasingly unfortunate adventures, Arabella is finally persuaded to give up her absurd 'Notions and Expectations' by Doctor——, who tells her:

> You have yet had little Opportunity of knowing the Ways of Mankind, which cannot be learned but from Experience, and of which the highest Understanding, and the lowest, must enter the World in equal Ignorance. I have lived long in a public Character, and have thought it my Duty to study those whom I have undertaken to admonish or instruct. (p. 379)

While a woman certainly would not wish to have a 'public Character', Lennox's implication is clear: some experience of the world is advisable, even necessary for a young woman. But too much knowledge of the world is not, as is evident in the portrayal of Mary Crawford in Austen's *Mansfield Park*, where Mary's worldly acceptance of Maria and Henry's adultery shocks Edmund so profoundly that he cannot then even consider loving her again.

In addition to the issue of 'worldly knowledge', Jane Austen also revisits the question of accomplishments in *Mansfield Park*. Maria and Julia Bertram are educated at home by a governess. When their cousin Fanny arrives from Portsmouth, they unkindly despise her precisely because she lacks the surface accomplishments that they have been taught to prize. She cannot speak French, has only two sashes, and cannot play the piano. Austen's comic list of the eclectic knowledge that Maria and Julia consider essential—'the difference between water-colours and crayons [...] the chronological order of the kings of England, with the dates of their accession, and most of the principal events of their reigns [...] the Roman emperors as low as Severus; besides a great deal of the Heathen Mythology, and all the Metals, Semi-Metals, Planets, and distinguished philosophers'—nicely illustrates the governess Miss Lee's failure to inculcate really useful moral and spiritual knowledge, and her focus on the superficial (Austen, 2005 [1814], pp. 20–21). We see here, then, that domestic education does not necessarily guard against the faults of privileging the external over the internal, as the conduct books suggest. As the novel progresses, it becomes clear that Maria and Julia's surface polish is actually positively harmful to them, since it allows them to *appear* good, while actually remaining selfish and vain:

> The Miss Bertrams were now fully established among the belles of the neighbourhood; and as they joined to beauty and brilliant acquirements a manner naturally easy, and carefully formed to general civility and obligingness, they possessed its favour as well as its admiration. Their vanity was in such good order that they seemed to be quite free from it, and gave themselves no airs; while the praises attending such behaviour, secured and brought round by their aunt, served to strengthen them in believing they had no faults. (p. 40)

Austen thus goes further than many other writers in figuring accomplishments not simply as pointless, but as actively destructive. Austen's *Mansfield Park* is, in fact, a particularly sustained intervention into the debates about the status of a domestic education, challenging a number of the assumptions made about its superiority. Maria, Julia and Fanny are all educated at home, by a governess. Lady Bertram, who technically has the main charge of their education, devolves it to Miss Lee and Mrs Norris. This is an error often commented on in conduct literature. Hannah More writes, for example, in her *Strictures on the Modern System of Female Education* (1799):

> Hired teachers are also under a disadvantage resembling tenants at rack-rent; it is their interest to bring in an immediate revenue of praise and profit, and, for the sake of a present rich crop, those who are not strictly conscientious, do not care how much the ground is impoverished for future produce. But parents, who are the lords of the soil, must look to permanent value, and to continued fruitfulness. (More, 1801 [1799], vol. 1, p. 97)[2]

Professional teachers are thus represented as being overly motivated by self-interest, while parents are described as having much more serious and virtuous motivations. Austen clearly agrees with the conduct literature here; in *Mansfield Park*, the total abnegation of responsibility by Maria and Julia's mother has bad consequences. Maria and Julia are petted and flattered by their aunt, they learn superficial accomplishments but fail to acquire humility, compassion, kindness or principle. Towards the end of the novel, their father, Sir Thomas, comes to realise that he has failed his daughters. As in *A Simple Story*, readers are asked to reflect on what constitutes 'a proper education' and Austen dedicates quite some time to this:

> [Sir Thomas] saw how ill he had judged, in expecting to counteract what was wrong in Mrs. Norris by its reverse in himself; clearly saw that he had but increased the evil by teaching them to repress their spirits in his presence so as to make their real disposition unknown to him [...]
>
> Here had been grievous mismanagement; but, bad as it was, he gradually grew to feel that it had not been the most direful mistake in his plan of education. Something must have been wanting *within*, or time would have worn away much of its ill effect. He feared that principle, active principle, had been wanting; that they had never been properly taught to govern their inclinations and tempers by that sense of duty which can alone suffice. They had been instructed theoretically in their religion, but never required to bring it into daily practice. To be distinguished for elegance and accomplishments, the authorised object of their youth, could have had no useful influence that way, no moral effect on the mind. He had meant them to be good, but his cares had been directed to the understanding and manners, not the disposition; and of the necessity of self-denial and humility, he feared they had never heard from any lips that could profit them.
>
> [...] Wretchedly did he feel, that with all the cost and care of an anxious and expensive education, he had brought up his daughters without their understanding their first duties, or his being acquainted with their character and temper. (Austen, 2005 [1814], pp. 535–536)

In this long passage, Austen clearly shows her readers that even 'an anxious and expensive' domestic education does not necessarily give a woman all she might need to live a virtuous moral life in the world as it is currently constituted: 'Something must have been wanting *within*'. On one level, this is a straightforward criticism of an 'authorised' education directed at forming external manners instead of internal principle—it is simply an extension of the criticism of 'accomplishments' education. But there is more to this passage than first meets the eye. Sir Thomas blames himself, but there is a strong suggestion, too, that children can be deceitful —Maria and Julia swiftly learn to act; to show Sir Thomas what he wishes to see, rather than being transparent and truthful. Austen therefore shows us that mere seclusion from the 'world' does not guarantee innocence and purity of mind.

This passage also reminds us of the disciplinary functions of education; the need to 'govern' and 'require' if students are to learn, thus opposing itself to Rousseau's popular doctrine of natural learning. Elsewhere in *Mansfield Park* this is made explicit in an even bleaker vision of how human beings learn best:

> [Tom] was the better for ever for his illness. He had suffered, and he had learned to think: two advantages that he had never known before; [...] He became what he ought to be: useful to his father, steady and quiet, and not living merely for himself. (p. 534)

Austen's view that suffering is an 'advantage' may strike us as callous, but the idea that it is a necessary part of education is not that unusual in the period. Mary Brunton also suggests in *Discipline* (1814) that 'the iron grasp of adversity' trains the mind in ways that a gentler domestic education cannot:

> If to such culture as this I owed the seeds of my besetting sins [pride and wilfulness], at least, it must be owned that the soil was propitious, for the bitter root spread with disastrous vigour; striking so deep, that the iron grasp of adversity, the giant strength of awakened conscience, have failed to tear it wholly from the heart, though they have crushed its outward luxuriance. (Brunton, 1986 [1814], p. 4)

And suffering is, of course, what differentiates Lady Matilda from her mother, Miss Milner, in *A Simple Story*:

> Educated in the school of adversity, and inured to retirement from her infancy, she had acquired a taste for all those amusements which a recluse life affords.—She was fond of walking and riding—was accomplished in the arts of music and drawing, by the most careful instructions of her mother—and as a scholar she excelled most of her sex, from the great pains Sandford had taken with that part of her education, and the great abilities he possessed for the task. (Inchbald, 1967 [1791], p. 221)

It is hard to reconcile the notion that 'adversity' is the 'school' that best allows a woman to excel that so frequently reoccurs in such novels, with the simultaneous insistent emphasis on protecting children and young women from the pernicious influences of the outside world, and the eighteenth-century assumption that girls would be best educated at home.[3] Through such commentaries on domestic education, therefore, writers like Brunton, Inchbald and Austen covertly suggest that in fact women must have a place in the public or external sphere if they are to develop the characters of moral worth that are so essential to the safety and security of the nation, and the education of future generations.[4]

In 1799, Hannah More, advocating 'a patriotism at once firm and feminine' exhorts the women of Britain, by amending their own morals and manners, 'to come forward and contribute their full and fair proportion towards the saving of their country' (More, 1801 [1799], vol. 1, p. 4). After reading history, Jane West suggests, women will 'rise from the perusal with a virtuous determination not to accelerate the ruin of our country' (West, 1996 [1811], p. 428). If a woman's moral taste is created and developed by what she reads, as West and others suggest, in periods of rising doubt and insecurity, the ways in which she is educated must therefore come under greater scrutiny. And if we take seriously the argument that the future of the nation lies in educating its women (an argument used by every writer of conduct books that I have cited), then that education takes on a new importance. What is at stake is thus not just a contested ideal of femininity, but a hope that a new generation of women, their taste formed by reading that is 'well-chosen and properly regulated' (Chapone, 1996 [1773], p. 187), to use Hester

Chapone's phrase, will reconstruct the morals and manners of the nation of England. As Jacques du Boscq wrote, more than a century earlier, 'I cannot chuse but think, that the Glory and Worth, and Happiness of any Nation depends as much upon [Women] as upon the Men' (du Boscq, 2002 [1632], p. 16). The fictions discussed here certainly do not all subscribe to this idea, but they do participate in a number of discussions related to it, as we have seen. For Austen, Haywood, Burney, Inchbald, Brunton, Wollstonecraft and Hays, as well as for Defoe, the many questions surrounding the role of women in the nation could be most satisfactorily worked out in fiction. 'Education' becomes a convenient floating signifier in these novels, deployed in ways that reflect a much broader concern about women's changing roles in the public and private spheres. The contradictions and complexities of the home/school debates over education should thus be seen as an extension of the contradictory attitudes that simultaneously extolled the importance of women as the mothers and educators of the nation and denied them any real access to political power.

Fictional discussions of domestic pedagogy thus interrogate the early eighteenth-century assumption that only a domestic education could properly prepare a woman for matrimony, or indeed for her future life. They enter vigorously into the question of what an accomplished woman might look like. They expose the inconsistencies in the arguments for a wholly private domestic education, just as they make fictional capital of the limitations of a public, or boarding-school education. In order to make the argument that a woman's education was vital to the public welfare of the nation, writers from Mary Wollstonecraft to Jane Austen were shifting the grounds of the debate, making the previously private into a matter of public concern. In so doing, the early eighteenth-century ideals of domestic education, which kept women firmly in the private sphere, began to seem outdated.

Acknowledgements

The author owes debts of gratitude to Christina de Bellaigue, Charlotte Bennett, Maxine Branagh, Michèle Cohen, Gillian Dow, Matthew Grenby, Emma MacLeod and the anonymous peer reviewers of the *ORE*, all of whom have shaped this article in positive ways.

Disclosure statement

No potential conflict of interest was reported by the author.

Notes

1. For a full discussion of the ways in which the new 'sentimental family' developed during the period, see Caroline Gonda, *Reading Daughters' Fiction 1709–1834* (1996), and Linda Colley's discussion of the role played by women in public life in *Britons* (1992, pp. 237–280). See also William St Clair's *The Reading Nation in the Romantic Period* (2004) for a discussion of the dissemination of texts.

2. The dangers of giving an inappropriate person control of a child's mind is discussed or illustrated in a number of earlier novels, perhaps most famously in Henry Fielding's *Tom Jones* (1749), in which the opposing philosophies and practice of Tom Jones' tutors Thwackum and Square are directly harmful to Tom's intellectual and moral development. Similarly, in *Betsy Thoughtless*, being removed from a harmful boarding school is a mixed blessing for Betsy—her new guardian, Lady Mellasin, is 'a very unfit person to have the care of youth, especially those of her own sex' (Haywood, 1997 [1751], p. 17).
3. A Christian emphasis on the necessity for battling against sin is no doubt at work here, but this does not seem enough to me to explain these scenes in their entirety.
4. In addition, such plots provide validation for fiction writers struggling to make the case for the respectability and moral worth of the new genre of the novel, who can argue that by an act of imaginative sympathy, a young woman can learn the lessons of suffering through reading, rather than through experience. Many of the justifications of fiction of the eighteenth century rely on an implicit or explicit appeal to this logic, and both the multitudes of suffering heroines in eighteenth-century fiction (of whom the most famous is surely Samuel Richardson's Clarissa Harlowe), and the very structures of the form bear tribute to its power. Such discussions of the importance of adversity in education thus play their part not only in debates over education, but in the ideological coding of the novel genre itself.

References

Aikin, J. (1796 [1793]). *Letters from a father to his son on various topics, related to literature and the conduct of life. Written in the years 1792 & 1793*. London: J. Johnson.

Aikin, J., & Barbauld, L. (1792–1794). *Evenings at home; or, The juvenile budget*. 4 vols. London: T. Johnson.

Anon. (1794). *The whole duty of woman; or, A complete system of female morality*. London: J. Wallis.

Anon. (1817). *The new female instructor; or, Young woman's guide to domestic happiness*. London: Thomas Kelly.

Argyle, A. (1743). *Instructions to a son, containing rules of conduct in publick and private life, written 1660 during his confinement*. Glasgow: R. Foulis, & Edinburgh: Hamilton & Balfour.

Armstrong, N. (1987). The rise of the domestic woman. In N. Armstrong & L. Tennenhouse (Eds.), *The ideology of conduct: Essays on literature and the history of sexuality* (pp. 96–141). New York & London: Methuen.

Astell, M. (1695). *A serious proposal to the ladies for the advancement of their true and greatest interest* ((2 ed. with corrections). London: Printed for R. Wilkin.

Austen, J. (2005 [1814]). *Mansfield Park*. (J. Wiltshire, Ed.). Cambridge: Cambridge University Press.

Austen, J. (2005 [1815]). *Emma*. ((R. Cronin & D. McMillan, Eds.). Cambridge: Cambridge University Press.
Bennett, J. (1787). *Strictures on female education; Chiefly as it relates to the culture of the heart, in four essays*. London: T. Cadell.
Bennett, J. (1789). *Letters to a young lady on a variety of useful and interesting subjects*. 2 vols. Warrington: W. Eyres.
Berquin, A. (1793). *The children's friend*. (L. Williams, Trans.). 6 vols. London: J. Stockdale et al.
Brunton, M. (1986 [1814]). *Discipline*. (F. Weldon, Ed.). London: Pandora Press.
Burney, F. (2000 [1778]). *Evelina, or, A young lady's entrance into the world*. (S. Kubica Howard, Ed.). Peterborough, ON: Broadview.
Bygrave, S. (2009). *Uses of education: Readings in enlightenment in England*. Lewisburg, PA: Bucknell University Press.
Caraccioli, L-A. (1786). *Advice from a lady of quality to her children; in the last stage of a lingering illness*. (S. Glasse, Trans.) (4th ed.). Gloucester: R. Raikes.
Chapone, H. (1996 [1773]). *Letters on the improvement of the mind, addressed to a young lady*. In J. Todd (Ed.), *Female education in the age of enlightenment*, vol. II. London: Pickering & Chatto.
Chapone, H. (1777). *A letter to a new-married lady*. London: E. & C. Dilly and J. Walter.
Chesterfield, P. D. S. (1799 [1774]). *Advice to his son, on men and manners* (7th ed.). London: W.J. and J. Richardson.
Cleland, J. (2005 [1751]). *Memoirs of a coxcomb*. (H. Gladfelder, Ed.). Peterborough, ON: Broadview.
Cohen, M. (2004). Gender and the private/public debate on education in the long eighteenth century. In R. Aldrich (Ed.), *Public or private education: Lessons from history* (pp. 15–35). London: Woburn Press.
Colley, L. (1992). *Britons: Forging the nation 1707–1837*. New Haven & London: Yale University Press.
Darwin, E. (1974 [1794–1796]). *Zoonomia*. (T. Verhase & P.R. Bindler, Eds.). 2 vols. New York: A.M.S. Press, Inc.
Darwin, E. (1797). *A plan for the conduct of female education in boarding schools*. Derby: J. Johnson.
Davies, R. (2014). *Written maternal authority and eighteenth-century education in Britain: Educating by the Book*. Farnham: Ashgate.
Defoe, D. (2004 [1722]). *Moll Flanders*. (A. J. Rivero, Ed.). New York: Norton.
du Boscq, J. (2002 [1632]). *The excellent woman*, Part 1. (T. Dorrington, Trans.). In W. St Clair & I. Maassen (Eds.), *Conduct literature for women, 1640–1710* (pp. 1–340). London: Pickering & Chatto.
Edgeworth, M. (1795). *Letters for literary ladies*. London: J. Johnson.
Edgeworth, M., & Edgeworth, R. L. (1996 [1798]). *Practical education*. (J. Wordsworth, Ed.). 3 vols. New York, NY: Woodstock Books.
Essex, J. (1722). *The young ladies conduct or, Rules for education, under several heads; with instructions upon DRESS, both before and after marriage*. London: John Brotherton.
Fénelon, M. (1753). *Instructions for the education of a daughter*. (G. Hickes, Trans.). Dublin: P. Wilson, J. Exchaw, and M. Williamson.
Fielding, H. (1996 [1749]), *Tom Jones*. (J. Bender & S. Stern, Eds.). Oxford: Oxford University Press.
Fordyce, J. (1766). *Sermons for young women*. 2 vols. London: A. Millar & T. Cadell.
Genlis, S-F. de. (1792). *Lessons of a governess to her pupils*. 3 vols. London: G.G.J. and J. Robinson.
Gisborne, T. (1789). *The principles of moral philosophy investigated, and briefly applied to the constitution of civil society*. London: B. White & Son.
Gisborne, T. (1794). *An enquiry into the duties of men in the higher and middle classes of society in Great Britain*. London: J. Davis.

Gisborne, T. (1996 [1797]). *An enquiry into the duties of the female sex.* In J. Todd (Ed.), *Female education in the age of enlightenment*, vol. II. London: Pickering & Chatto.

Gonda, C. (1996). *Reading daughters' fiction 1709–1834.* Cambridge: Cambridge University Press.

Gregory, J. (1795 [1761]). *A father's legacy to his daughters.* London: W. Lane.

Halifax, G. S. (1724 [1688]). *The lady's new-year's-gift: or Advice to a daughter* (10th ed.). Dublin: A. Rhames.

Hays, M. (1996 [1796]). *Memoirs of Emma Courtney.* (E. Ty, Ed.). Oxford: Oxford World's Classics.

Haywood, E. (1997 [1751]). *The history of Miss Betsy Thoughtless.* (B. Fowkes Tobin, Ed.). Oxford: Oxford World's Classics.

Hunter, R. (1776). *Advice from a father to his son just entered into the army and about to go abroad into action. In seven letters.* London: J. Johnson.

Inchbald, E. (1967 [1791]). *A simple story.* (J. M. S. Tompkins, Ed.). London: Oxford University Press.

Knox, V. (1781). *Liberal education: or, A practical treatise on the methods of acquiring useful and polite learning.* London: Charles Dilly.

Lennox, C. (2008 [1752]). *The female Quixote.* (M. Dalziel, Ed. with an introduction by M.A. Doody). Oxford: Oxford World Classics.

Locke, J. (1693). *Some thoughts concerning education.* London: printed for A. and J. Churchill.

Macaulay Graham, C. (1790). *Letters on education.* London: C. Dilly.

Makin, B. (2002 [1673]). *An essay to revive the antient education of gentlewomen.* In W.St Clair & I.Massen (Eds), *Conduct literature for women, 1640–1710: Volume 2.* London: Pickering & Chatto.

Moir, J. (1786 [1784]). *Female tuition; or, An address to mothers on the education of daughters* (2nd ed.). London: John Murray.

Monro, A. (1996). 'The professor's daughter: An essay on female conduct' transcribed with introduction and notes by P. A. G. Monro M.D. *Proceedings of the Royal College of Physicians of Edinburgh*, 26, 1.

More, H. (1801 [1799]). *Strictures on the modern system of female education.* 2 vols (9th ed.). London: T. Cadell and W. Davies.

More, H. (1995 [1808]). *Cœlebs in search of a wife.* (M. Waldron, Ed.). Bristol: Thoemmes Press.

Murry, A. (1779). *Mentoria: or The young ladies' instructor, in familiar conversations on moral and entertaining subjects calculated to improve young minds, in the essential as well as ornamental part of female education.* Dublin: Price, Sheppard [...] & Watson.

Pearson, J. (1999). *Women's reading in Britain 1750–1835.* Cambridge: Cambridge University Press.

Rousseau, J. J. (1913 [1762]). *Émile.* London: J.M. Dent.

Sheridan, T. (1756). *British education: Or the source of the disorders of Great Britain.* Dublin: George Faulkner.

St Clair, W. (2004). *The reading nation in the Romantic period.* Cambridge: Cambridge University Press.

Wakefield, P. (1995 [1794–1797]). *Mental improvement.* (A. B. Shteir, Ed.). East Lansing: Colleagues Press.

Wakefield, P. (1805). *Domestic recreation, or, Dialogues illustrative of natural and scientific subjects* London: Printed for Darnton and Harvey.

West, J. (1996 [1811]). *Letters to a young lady, vol. II.* In J. Todd (Ed.), *Female education in the age of enlightenment*, vol. V. London: Pickering & Chatto.

Wollstonecraft, M. (1994 [1787]). *Thoughts on the education of daughters.* Oxford & New York: Woodstock Books.

Wollstonecraft, M. (1979 [1789]). *The female reader.* (M. Ferguson, Ed.). Delmar, NY: Scholars' Facsimiles & Reprints.
Wollstonecraft, M. (1992 [1792]). *A vindication of the rights of Woman.* London: Everyman.
Woodley, S. (2009). 'Oh miserable and most ruinous measure': The debate between private and public education in Britain, 1760–1800. In M. Hilton & J. Shefrin (Eds.), *Educating the child in Enlightenment Britain: Beliefs, cultures, practices* (pp. 21–39). Farnham: Ashgate.
Zaczek, B. M. (1997). *Censored sentiments: Letters and censorship in epistolary novels and conduct material.* Newark, DE: University of Delaware Press.

The pedagogy of conversation in the home: 'familiar conversation' as a pedagogical tool in eighteenth and nineteenth-century England

Michèle Cohen
Richmond University and UCL Institute of Education, University of London, UK

This article argues that domestic conversations taking place in a sociable context played a more important role than has hitherto been considered in the intellectual training and development of children. The centrality of conversation as an informal method of training the mind to reason had one important consequence: the publication of the highly successful 'familiar format', texts which used 'conversation' as the method of instruction. Written mainly but not exclusively by women, these texts were modelled on the instructive 'familiar' conversations which were part of the fabric of social and familial exchanges, and were an attempt to extend conversation's educational effectiveness into a pedagogy. The article also explores why the format became a lost pedagogy.

By the middle of the eighteenth century, the home was increasingly seen as the privileged site, 'the best place' (Walters, 1997, p. 131) for instructional activities. Although domestic education had long been the norm for very young children, for most girls and for many boys in upper class and middling professional families, this perception of the home as the ideal site for instruction suggests a shift not just in the meaning of the home but in the meaning of education. In this period, the domestic space became the preferred site for the diffusion and consumption of knowledge. What was new, in addition, is that it involved the 'entire family' (Secord, 1985, p. 133; see also Keene, 2014). Home education could be envisaged because, in the absence of an overall educational authority and of any teacher training, anyone could teach, and often did (Cohen, 2006). Moreover, because the classical curriculum was relatively fixed and unchanging, a classically educated father could teach his son what he had learned as well as a schoolmaster could. 'You are in every respect qualified for the task of instructing your son, and preparing him for the university', poet William Cowper wrote to his friend the Rev William Unwin. In the case of girls, whose education was 'modern' (in the sense of not being 'classical'), there was no standard curriculum and a parent (usually a mother, but in some cases a father) could teach what they had learned as well as a governess or schoolmistress would. In this period, the relative ease with which home education could be conducted was coupled with an emphasis on domestic instruction as preferable not only for girls, but also for boys. Thus, Cowper underlined his point by adding that at school, a boy's 'morals are sure to be but little attended to' whereas a home education ensures boys are under the watchful eye of their father (Cowper, 1827 [17 September 1780], p. 90) and thus 'escape the dangers of "the tavern, the gaming table or the brothel"' (Secord, 1985, p. 129).

Education within the family however also provided an additional attraction, overlooked by most histories of education: familiar conversation. The conversations held by families and their social circle, which could include a variety of guests, could broaden children's horizons.

Being able to converse well on a wide range of subjects including natural history, chemistry, mineralogy and botany ensured that a guest would be 'particularly esteemed' (Gleadle, 2003, p. 64). Contemporaries had much to say about the role conversation played in developing not just knowledge but the mind and critical faculties. This is because 'conversation' was not just talk. Not only was culture 'a form of conversation', but at the time conversation was also involved in issues ranging from how it should be performed to whether it could represent 'a community of culture', be a form of 'sober enquiry after truth' or a 'reminder of linguistic dispersal and potentially of social disintegration' (Mee, 2011, pp. 7, 122, 237). Conversation was also an integral part of practices of sociability and politeness aimed at individual improvement and self fashioning, and had to be instructive as well as entertaining. Author of conduct literature Hester Chapone captured the essence of this ideal in her 'Essay on Conversation' where she notes that 'It is almost impossible that an evening should pass in mutual endeavours to entertain each other [in conversation], without something being struck out, that would, in some degree enlighten and improve the mind' (Chapone, 1775, p. 16).

In the late eighteenth century then, conversation was of central importance both as a key element of sociability and as a central feature of domestic instruction. The aim of this article is to investigate the ways middle class and elite families exploited conversation in both its oral and written modes—spoken conversations and texts constructed as 'conversations'—as a means of educating their children at home. I argue that the thoughtful and deliberate use of familiar conversation, with its potential for formality as well as informality, digressions, interruptions and for entertainment as well as 'improvement', made the domestic space a key site for the training of children's minds and critical faculties.

HOME EDUCATION IN HISTORICAL PERSPECTIVE

I. Conversation at home

Eighteenth-century parents were aware of the importance of conversation in the training of children's minds. For example, in her diary, Anna Larpent, the wife of a civil servant and mother of two sons, noted on 30 October 1792:

> Heard George (aged 6) English and Latin lessons, he read in Sandford and Merton [although?] the scenery of which was at Venice and in Turkey. This raised his geographical enquiries. He placed the map of Europe, found the places named and had much general conversation concerning the map of [C?] which fitted up all our time, perhaps more usefully than by our routine of learning. (Larpent, 30 October 1792)

Similarly, the educationist Maria Edgeworth's comment that 'whatever can be taught in conversation, is clear gain in instruction' (Edgeworth & Edgeworth, 1798/1801, vol. II, p. 53) leaves no doubt that she was a firm believer in the importance of conversation, not as random desultory talk, but as a system. In the same vein, in the anonymous *Thoughts on Domestic Education* (1826) 'A Mother' states that: 'the best aim of education is to teach children to think for themselves', emphasising conversation as the means to do so. She describes her method: 'on reading Defoe's admirable story of Robinson Crusoe, the young reader might easily be led into a familiar chat respecting the conduct of its hero ... and a consciousness of [it] could be insensibly awakened in the mind' (A Mother, 1826, p. 45). By the 1830s, the idea of teaching children 'without their suspecting it' by using familiar conversation was common place (Genlis, 2007 [1783], p. 250). Thus, Thomas Shore, a country clergyman and educator, was reported in his daughter's diary as arguing that the reason poor children seemed to have 'more vacancy and stupidity of mind than those of the higher ranks' was not because of a 'natural want of intelligence' but, he explained, 'because they are not drawn out by questions; they are not in the habit of being taught to apply what they know' (Shore, 1891 [26 March 1833], p. 40). 'Drawing out by questions' was the quintessential characteristic of instructive conversation, formal and informal, spoken and written; it was what educationists *did*, when they used conversation to instruct. Drawing children out by questions ensured that they were actively involved—asking as well as answering questions, agreeing as well as disagreeing, interrupting and changing the subject—their voices were foregrounded. It was also the pedagogical model for the 'familiar format', texts structured as 'conversations' which I will discuss below.

II. The acquisition of conversation skills

Although there has been no systematic study of children's participation in the sociable activities of middle class and elite circles, Peter Borsay has argued that children as young as six or seven were included in the leisure activities of their families (Borsay, 2006). While he does not specify the kind of activities this leisure included, there is much evidence to suggest that in middle and upper class families, children's participation in social/domestic conversations with adults was a normal feature of their upbringing.

Children's language socialisation involves not just learning language but also what to say, how and when to say it (Hymes, 1972). As a result, home education included training in manners, which eighteenth-century middling and elite families considered an integral part of upbringing. Exercising children's minds *by* conversation was indivisible from training and disciplining their tongue *for* conversation, as required by the conventions of politeness and sociability. The complex skills comprising conversation were neither 'natural' nor simple, as attested by the numerous manuals of conversation published in the late eighteenth century. They were primarily acquired in 'good', mainly adult, company. It was in company, argues Ingrid Tague, that elite boys and girls shared 'the same educational process' in the 'informal, yet essential, lessons of sociability' (Tague, 2002).

Evidence from gentry and middle class families in this period reveals many instances of parents advocating exposure to adult society and conversation as a means of training in manners. Thus Mrs Delany's advice to her sister to expose her little daughter to a 'variety of good company, which is of more use in forming a gracious manner from the ages of seven to fourteen than seven years after that', conveys how important she considers this training to be (Delany, 1861 [letter of 7 April 1754], 1st ser., vol. 3, p. 219). Similarly, when Lord Sheffield encouraged his daughter Maria Josepha, while yet a child, to enter into all his interests, and converse with 'the leading men' he entertained at his home, he was not just enabling 'her keen intellect' to be stimulated (Adeane, 1896, p. xvii) but implicitly ensured that she would know how to express her opinions. Maria Josepha was not unusual. Such lessons were also valued for boys, and many boys participated, like girls, in domestic conversation and instruction, but evidence about their participation is harder to find than for girls. The reason is mainly historiographical. Education, as regards boys, usually refers to their learning the classics and less formal instruction has tended to be overlooked. However, there are some significant examples. Thus Lady Stafford deplored the absence of her 14 year old son Granville at a dinner she hosted where Prime Minister Pitt explicated Homer in a 'lively and entertaining' manner (Leveson Gower, G. letter of 14 May 1787, in Castalia, 1916, vol. 1, p. 8). Granville's participation in learned table talk with eminent personages was normal in their family. Texts in the familiar format also demonstrate clearly that boys, as well as girls, engaged in domestic conversations on a variety of subjects.

Advice about conversation included in most eighteenth-century conduct books and prescriptive educational texts usually linked its intellectual and social skills. In *The Polite Lady; or a Course of Female Education* published in 1775, the letter 'Portia' writes to her daughter at boarding school advising her to practise conversation nicely illustrates this: conversation, 'Portia' writes, will 'whet your genius and fix your attention, warm and improve your heart, polish and refine your manners, and give you a certain ease and elegance of address which is not to be obtained in any other way' ([Allen], 1775, p. 153). Such sentiments were echoed in many other advice texts. For conversations to 'whet the genius' or 'stimulate the intellect', they had to be instructive, but the evanescence of the spoken word makes it impossible for the historian to reach, and to assess how far such advice was put into practice.

Letters are one of the ways of recovering conversations as letter writers often recorded them (see Hannan, 2013), and they do suggest that conversation was frequently used in these ways. Reading, often done aloud, was inextricably intertwined with active listening and critical judgement, all important skills necessary for conducting polite conversation and therefore necessary components of children's education. In the Edgeworth household, children would practise them by being 'encouraged to ask questions' during reading sessions (Butler, 1972, p. 99). Similarly, when John Aikin was writing *Evenings at Home*, a juvenile collection intended for family reading aloud, he 'would have everything he wrote read aloud by one member of the family to the others, and encouraged comments even from the youngest' (Rogers, 1958, p. 122). Familial conversations about reading were thus an important means of putting into practice Locke's pedagogical assertion that 'the object of education is to inculcate in children the practice of deliberation' so that they will be able to think rationally and consider 'whether to assent propositions about the physical, intellectual, moral and political worlds' (Parry, 2007, p. 218). These practices also rehearsed the skills of conversation itself. Indeed, the reading cards and other material artefacts Jane Johnson, a clergyman's wife, developed in the 1740s to teach her children to read, were 'designed not only for learning to read but also to become skilled in the art of conversation as well as the art of reading aloud—signs of good manners and gentility' (Arizpe & Styles, 2004, p. 344).

For all the expansion of print, the eighteenth century was still very much an oral culture (Secord, 2007) especially as the practice of politeness was indissolubly linked to conversation, its 'master metaphor' (Cohen, 1996; Eger, 2005; Klein, 1994, p. 8). A critical component of conversation as well as polite practice concerned the necessity to pay attention to what people said and retain what they said. This required a 'habit of attention' as well as memory, which children were trained to develop from a young age by practising listening to conversations or readings and then recounting them orally or by writing them down from memory. This was so thoroughly inculcated that eighteenth-century adults remembered conversations and therefore learned by conversation in ways that we can perhaps imagine but no longer experience. Elizabeth Robinson attended the learned conversations hosted by her step-grandfather Conyers Middleton who then expected her to provide an account of these conversations (Robinson, 1930 [1801]). Even though Middleton thought this reporting might be difficult as she was not yet in her teens, he thought she would thus acquire a 'habit of attention' that would be of use to her in the future (Doran, 1873, p. 4). Like letters, diaries and journals can provide evidence of the role and practice of conversation in self-instruction. Naturalist and artist Katherine Plymley's diaries include 'lengthy political conversations she had witnessed between her brother and his guests' which she wrote down and 'elaborated upon', explaining their meanings (Gleadle, 2003, pp. 68–70). Plymley was deploying her mastery of a skill she was likely to have learned when young, to extend her self-education.

Such skills and strategies were fostered by the pedagogical strategies then adopted in the home. For, contrary to the common historiographical assumption that domestic education was superficial, usually 'haphazard' and 'nearly always unsystematic' (Bryant, 1985, pp. 17–18; Hilton & Shefrin, 2009, p. 9; Sutherland, 2000, p. 31), in the eighteenth century, the instruction offered to girls at home might be extensive. Thus, while there was no prescribed curriculum for girls' education, and every individual parent, moralist, educationist, schoolmistress or girl herself could devise their own curriculum, and often did (see Cohen, 2006), there was a core curriculum which usually included history, geography, religion and languages such as French and Italian, as well as 'accomplishments' such as music and dancing (Cohen, 2004, 2005b, 2006). In addition, affluent homes might often also provide a well-furnished library (Allan, 2008; Pearson, 1999), which daughters might use—as Catharine Macaulay and Jane Austen did—to great effect. In contrast, Eliza Fletcher, who had read Addison in her father's library before attending school from the age of 11 in the 1780s, found that 'four volumes of the *Spectator* constituted our whole school library' (Fletcher, 1874, p. 18). The instruction offered at home might often be better than anything most schools of the time could offer.

This was arguably true for boys as well. Thus, in a letter to Unwin, William Cowper remarks that 'geography, a science ... necessary to the accomplishment of a gentleman, yet ... imperfectly, if at all, inculcated in schools' (Cowper, 1827, [7 September 1780], p. 88). The notoriously narrow classical curriculum of boys' schools (see Stray, 1998) could however be supplemented by home instruction. Significantly, both girls' home education and the complementary instruction offered to boys were facilitated by the expansion of juvenile publishing for young readers (Secord, 1985), in particular, of dialogic texts in 'familiar' format. These texts aimed to emulate the instructive conversations that were part of the fabric of the familial exchanges documented in the letters and memoirs discussed so far.

The dialogic texts which have attracted most scholarly attention are those which 'popularised' science (Amies, 1985; Fyfe, 2000a, 2000b, 2008; Gates, 1998; Hilton, 2007; Keene, 2014; Myers 1989, 1997; Secord, 1985; Shteir 1996), but I argue that the familiar format, just like these conversations, was used to teach a variety of subjects ranging from history, both sacred and secular, and English grammar to painting and domestic duties to young married women.

III. The familiar format

Although texts in familiar format are instructional, they are not always constructed as a didactic exchange between an all-knowing adult-teacher and an ignorant child-learner (Myers, 1989; Shteir, 1996). Rather, the characters can include two or more children or adolescents who may or may not be siblings, teaching each other and conversing with an adult who is neither all-knowing nor always in control of the dialogues and may just be a secondary character, or even in the absence of adults (see Jamieson, 1819), and the form in which knowledge is provided and discussed is not necessarily formulaic and fixed, as G. Myers and Ann Shteir have argued (Myers, 1989; Shteir, 1996). To illustrate this variety, I have selected four excerpts to show different positionings for 'learners' and 'teachers' as well as textual interruptions and digressions, two of the techniques authors used to better simulate conversational authenticity in the written mode (Pujol, 2005). The first is an excerpt from *Conversations on Chemistry* (1806) by Jane Marcet, selected to show the relationship between the tutor, Mrs B, and one of her pupils, where the pupil queries Mrs B's statement, who then admits an error.

Conversation V 'On Oxygen and Nitrogen'

Mrs B	... the iron, in burning, has acquired exactly the weight of the oxygen which has disappeared, and is now combined with it. It has become oxide of iron.
Caroline:	I do not know what you mean by saying that the oxygen has disappeared, Mrs B, for it was always invisible.
Mrs B	True, my dear, the expression was incorrect. (Marcet, 1806, vol. I, pp. 140–141)

The second excerpt, from Alexander Jamieson's *Conversations on General History* (1819), exploits what Catherine Dille has shown to have been a domestic practice of the period, siblings instructing each other without an adult being present (Dille, 2013, July). In this text, the father appears only in the fifth conversation and is not the sole authority.

Henry	But Amelia, pray go on with your account of the sciences in ancient Egypt.
Amelia	In medicine the Egyptians made little progress, as anatomy was not studied anciently ... [she continues].
Henry	now I am satisfied
Charlotte	Indeed—and where now is your inquisitiveness about all the institutions of the Egyptians?
Amelia	not so, Charlotte: Listen to me, Henry:—About the priests, whose morality was pure and refined, though it has little influence on the manners of the people ... debased by the most absurd and contemptible superstitions ... [she continues]. (Jamieson, 1819, pp. 16–18)

The third excerpt, from Mrs Markham's *History of England*, exemplifies the different forms instructional conversations could take, and shows how the instructor, the mother, shifts the discussion to material not included in the text she has just read out because of the questions the children put to her.

Mrs M has just been discussing the battles of Cressy, Poitiers and Agincourt.

Richard:	Was it not extraordinary, mamma, that so small a number of English should again beat an immense army of French?
Mary:	I wish, mamma, there were not so many shocking stories in history.
Mrs M:	History is, indeed, a sad catalogue of human miseries, and one is glad to turn from the horrors of war and bloodshed to the tranquillity of private life. Shall I tell you something of the domestic habits of the English in the fifteenth century?
Mary:	Oh do, Mamma, I shall like that very much. (Markham, 1823, pp. 186–187)

The last excerpt is a counter-example: N. Meredith, *Rudiments of Chemical Philosophy* (1810), where there are no characters, and the dialogic format does not attempt to simulate a real conversation; Meredith warns the reader that he is not interested in emulating real conversations with characters each with their own voice: 'the dramatis personae of the text are not well supported', but this is 'of no consequence at all' because 'every one knows that the information or entertainment of the reader is the object aimed at' (Meredith, 1810, p. xiii).

What is the most general effect of caloric on the different bodies?

Its most general effect is the increase of their bulk; hence, if a bar of iron be accurately measured when cold, and afterwards heated, it will be found, if measured again while hot, to have increased in length.

Has caloric the same effect on fluid bodies as on solids?

Yes, but in a much greater degree, their particle being more easily separated from each other; everyone who knows the principle on which the steam engine is constructed, must be aware how much the bulk of water is increased, when converted into *steam* by its union with caloric .... (Meredith, 1810, pp. 5–6)

While conversation was always associated with the free exchange of ideas, it did not necessarily entail avoiding contention and debate. On the contrary, there was 'a role for combative talk as pleasurable and productive' (Mee, 2011, p. 5). For example, in John Aikin and Anna Barbauld's social circle, people 'exercised their right ... to examine, compare, choose, reject' (Mee, 2011, p. 122). Training children to think rationally and critically meant allowing them that right too. Marcet's *Conversations on Chemistry* include several instances where pupils disagree with or show up Mrs B's errors, as in the excerpt above. Equally significant is that in both Marcet's and Markham's excerpts, the interruptions and digressions all come from the children, demonstrating that they are not mere passive recipients, receptacles to be filled with knowledge. They are presented as agents, and their interruptions can shape the direction of the narrative. This is also how the familiar format, where both pupils and the teacher 'asked questions and advanced opinions' (Amies, 1985, p. 91; Fyfe, 2000a) differs from 'catechisms' where the pupil's sole role is to ask the questions that produce undeviatingly the knowledge to be conveyed, as shown in the excerpt from Meredith.

IV. Choosing the familiar format

Since other textual dialogic forms—'catechisms' and 'Questions and Answers' without characters—co-existed with the familiar format, why did authors choose to use the latter?

Evidence from within the texts themselves suggests a number of reasons. Thus, Priscilla Wakefield explained that she adopted the dialogue format for her *Mental Improvement*, because she wanted her instructive lessons to 'be read rather from choice than from compulsion, and be sought by my young readers, as an entertainment not shunned as a mere dry perceptive lesson' (Wakefield, 1794, vol. I, p. ii). Ann Murry, author of *Mentoria*, chose it for a different reason: it acts 'to lure the mind into knowledge, and imperceptibly conduct it to the goal of wisdom. This mode of practice often succeeds, where formal precept fails' (Murry, 1778, p. xi). Even though written conversations are nothing like spoken ones, authors using the conversational genre presented their work as if this difference did not matter, possibly because the shift from spoken to written mode was perceived as mere 'transcription' (Anon., 1823, p. 53). Like spoken conversation, it was an attractive and non-coercive mode of instruction for both sexes, particularly in contrast to the regime of rote learning prevailing in boys' schools (see however Grenby, 2009) and because conversation was a successful method for conveying knowledge without 'cramping' the mind. This is echoed in the work of today's leading psycholinguists, who emphasise the pedagogical effectiveness of mutually constructed knowledge through 'cumulative talk' between teacher and learner (Mercer & Littleton, 2007, p. 54). Wakefield further highlighted what might be another reason for its popularity, the familial and domestic aspect of conversational instruction, which chimed particularly well with a contemporary emphasis on parental intimacy and close relations between siblings. Encouraged by 'a new culture of open parental affection' (Grenby, 2011, p. 207), Wakefield argued that the 'familiar intercourse, that is now maintained with young people by their parents, and those who preside over their education' is a result of a shift from

> The austere manners of former times secluded children from the advantage of conversing with their parents or instructors; an unnatural distance was maintained between them; they were seldom admitted into the parlour, but to pay a ceremonious visit … The times are greatly altered in this respect for the better, and the familiar intercourse, that is now maintained with young people by their parents, and those who preside over their education, affords them an agreeable opportunity of enlarging their minds, and attaining a fund of knowledge, by the easy medium of conversation. (Wakefield, 1794, vol. I, pp. 119–120)

These texts also enacted Catharine Macaulay's recommendation for parents to 'take measures for the virtue and harmony of your family, by uniting their [children's] young minds early in the soft bonds of friendship' (Macaulay, 1790, Letter iv, p. 50) and bringing them up together. In *Natural History*, the father chides his son Charles: 'you need not have called your sister silly; you are twelve years old and she is but six. You should instruct her kindly and not ridicule her' (Rippingham, 1815, vol. 1, p. 12).

The domestic site also provided the opportunity to transform the quotidian into an educational experience. Maria Edgeworth noted in *Practical Education* that 'we have found, from experience, that an early knowledge of the first principles of science … may be insensibly acquired from the usual incidents of life' (Edgeworth & Edgeworth, 1798/1801, vol. II, p. vii). Mrs Mason, the moral governess in Wollstonecraft's familiar dialogues *Original Stories from Real Life*, 'converts everyday situations into her instructional medium—a bad habit, a passerby, a visit, a natural scene, a holiday festivity' (Myers, 1986, p. 46; Wollstonecraft, 1788).

HOME EDUCATION IN HISTORICAL PERSPECTIVE

The familiar format resonated very clearly with late eighteenth-century ideas about instructive conversation and contemporary pedagogical preferences. Spoken conversations developed children's critical thought, enlarged their mind and allowed the acquisition of knowledge at the same time as training them in the art of expressing their thoughts clearly in keeping with the requirements of polite sociability. The familiar genre allowed authors to extend the 'efficacy of conversation' (Fyfe, 2000a, p. 473) to a textual form. To achieve this aim, authors appropriated the conversations of social intercourse, expanded their form, infused them with their own pedagogical ideas and produced different educational experiences. Jane Marcet, one of the most celebrated writers of the genre, exploits this in a multilayered exchange in her *Conversations on the History of England*. Sophy, aged eight, wants to read the history book her brother Willy is reading. Her mother replies:

> The [history] your brother is reading is written by Mrs Markham: it is intended for children older than you are; it is fit for Willy, and Lady Callcott's is for you. But, mamma, Sophy says, what makes his history so amusing is the conversation at the end of every chapter: all the children talk about what they have been reading, and Mrs Markham explains what they do not understand. Is it so in this little history? No, replied her mother. But I will tell you how we can make up for that; we may talk the conversations instead of reading them. You must make your own observations, and I will explain the difficulties. (Marcet, 1842, pp. 1–3)

Whether aiming or just claiming to emulate real conversations, the genre flourished from the 1780s until the mid-nineteenth century. Through this genre, educators and authors developed pedagogies that were supremely well-adapted to the conversable sociabilities and family cultures of the late eighteenth century (see Hilton, 2007). It thrived in a period when domestic instruction was considered the ideal for both boys and girls, and continued to have currency in a period of moral as well as educational pressure on English middle and upper class families to educate daughters at home. Even though boarding school education expanded for both sexes in the late eighteenth and early nineteenth centuries (Skedd, 1997), domestic instruction with a mother, father or benevolent governess as instructor remained important well into the nineteenth century. Authors adopting the 'familiar format' simultaneously exemplified and enabled the practice.

Yet, by the 1850s, Barbara Gates argues, 'the dialogue form had begun to outlive its own credibility' (Gates, 1998, p. 43). It became a derogated pedagogy. While a number of suggestions have been put forward to explain why texts in familiar format became popular (Amies, 1985; Gates, 1998; G. Myers, 1989; M. Myers, 1986; Shteir, 1996), only Ann Shteir has proposed an explanation for its demise. In her study of women and botany, Shteir argues that dialogic texts to teach botany, often associated with women, became vulnerable to 'textual misogyny' in the later nineteenth century. This suited a professionalising agenda which aimed to distinguish between botany as a polite accomplishment embodied rhetorically 'feminine', and serious scientific botany for males (Shteir, 1996, pp. 163, 156). However, as Shteir discusses only those dialogic texts referring to botany, while the familiar format was used for a wider variety of subjects of instruction, her argument has limited explanatory power. Gender undoubtedly played a role, since women educators, who were the main writers of the familiar format, were under attack since the late eighteenth century (Clarke, 1997), but broader cultural changes also need to be taken into account.

V. The demise of the familiar format

Both the popularity and the demise of the familiar format can be explained by its relation to the role of spoken conversation in the practice of politeness and sociability in the long eighteenth century. Conversation was not just a pedagogy, it was an integral aspect of politeness, the practice that gave it meaning and for which it was the supreme expression. The familiar format was modelled on conversations that took place in the context of eighteenth-century polite sociability, but as this dominant cultural form waned in the early nineteenth century (Cohen, 2005a), conversation, no longer framed by politeness, could be abstracted from the practice of social skills and sociability and become just a method. As a method, 'conversation' could be—and was—appropriated for a wide variety of texts, ranging from dialogic with named characters, to third-person narratives with only reported speech, sometimes in the same text. Elizabeth Helme's *History of Scotland related in familiar conversations by a father to his children*, is an example of the latter. As read by the father, Mr Wilmot, the text is a narrative, even though it deploys 'interruptions' because, Helme argues in her introduction, they 'render[d] the subjects lighter, and the domestic conversations more interesting to the children' (Helme, 1804, p. vii). However, her interruptions are 'reported': 'Indeed papa', interrupted John ' it was more than he merited after what he had said' (Helme, 1804, p. 127) whereas the interruptions used in dialogic texts like Marcet's *Conversations on Chemistry*, to make conversations sound 'authentic', actually break the visual text:

Mrs B:	Oxygen gas is a little heavier than atmospherical air, therefore it will not mix with it very rapidly and, if I do not leave the opening uncovered, we shall not lose any—
Caroline:	Oh, what a brilliant and beautiful flame! (Marcet, 1806, vol. I, Conversation V, p. 139)

This difference could matter when the texts were read aloud, as they usually were (Fyfe, 1999, 2000b; Grenby, 2009, 2011).

The meaning of conversation as a method could also be stretched, as in Mrs Alfred Higginson's *The English Schoolgirl* (1859). This text consists of narrative 'lectures' on a variety of subjects, meant to form the basis for 'familiar and conversational weekly lessons' (Higginson, 1859, p. vii). Conversations are the justification for the book's existence and integral to its methodology, but they are putative, and take place *outside*, not *inside* the text. Such examples show how loosely the term 'conversation' could be used by the mid-nineteenth century, although they beg explanation as to why authors still claimed that 'conversation' was central to their methodology. One hypothesis is that advertising conversation as the instructional method had commercial appeal because it was 'one means of forming and elevating individual character' (Higginson, 1859, p. vii) and promised instructional success.

It was not just the meaning of conversation, however, that changed by the mid-nineteenth century, its role in social life was also changing. Earlier, knowing how to converse was essential and parents knew it was important for their children to acquire the expressive and intellectual skills associated with it for their future success. At the end of the eighteenth century, conversation was also developing another function, one which linked domestic familial instruction with what Priscilla Wakefield claimed was the 'new affection' in parents' relations to their children (Wakefield, 1794, vol. 1, pp. 119–120). Helme's *History of Scotland* illustrates the force of these idealised filial relations. Asked by his father what he wants as amusements for his birthday, John replies 'I had rather a thousand times be seated around our own fireside listening to either papa or [his mother], relating some history, as you did that of England' (Helme, 1804, p. 3).

As nothing more than a method, conversation could also be criticised, and was. In the late eighteenth century, Clergyman Joseph Robertson was already scorning the 'gossiping dialogue' and the 'trifling drama' (Robertson, 1798, p. 15) of the familiar format. Nearly 30 years later J. S. Forsyth, author of an introduction to Linnaeus, mocked dialogic texts as a 'baby system of education' fit to be taught only by 'some garrulous old woman or pedantic spinster' (Forsyth, 1827, pp. 15, 17). While these two examples illustrate Shteir's 'textual misogyny' (Shteir, 1996, p. 163), Robertson also targeted the 'slogan' (Grenby, 2003) of eighteenth-century pedagogy, that instruction be amusing and entertaining. He claimed that the 'business of education is a serious pursuit', not an amusement and that diverting children from the paths of science gave them a 'disrelish' for anything which is not amusing (Robertson, 1798, p. 11). His critique is evidence of an emerging trend which decried the entertaining aspect of 'serious' education (Arizpe & Styles, 2004). It would eventually result in the segregation of amusing and instructive texts. From the end of the nineteenth century 'new children's books were written to amuse children, while instruction was left to the schoolroom' (Fyfe, 1999, p. 28). This subverted the character of the dialogic format, its foundation in the conversational pedagogy of the eighteenth century. However it was not schooling as such which produced this change. In the late eighteenth century, in *Evenings at Home*, a paradigmatic instructional text, the readings and conversations take place after the school day, as do those in the later *Austin Hall*, and in *Breakfast Table Science* (Aikin & Barbauld, 1846 [1792–1796]; Anon., 1831; Wright, 1840). Even then, conversation in its late eighteenth-century social and pedagogical meanings was still central to instruction, as the author of *Austin Hall* declares in the 'preface to parents': 'It is by conversation, by daily intercourse, that character is chiefly formed. The Royal road to knowledge is that of oral communication … Familiar intercourse with our children is the best mode of education' (Anon., 1831, p. iii). As this text makes clear, familiar conversation was highly valued, even when it was supplementary to schooling.

And yet, one aspect of familiar conversation might have made it vulnerable to the charge of frivolity and lack of seriousness, and vulnerable to the claims to order and system being made by contemporary schools: its informal and digressive nature. The introduction of *Evenings at Home* specifies that its authors 'have presented its contents in the promiscuous order in which they came to hand, which they think will prove more agreeable than a methodical arrangement' (Aikin & Barbauld, 1846 [1792–1796], p. 8), although this was planned by the authors (Fyfe, 1999). The 'promiscuous' topics of the delightful *Breakfast Table Science* include amusing questions such as 'Why our dog's teeth are white', 'Why a rotten apple is bitter', 'if a fly had a sore toe, what would happen', all of which convey serious scientific information but lack any discernible order in their presentation. Such promiscuity was highly prized in the sociable conversation of the late eighteenth century. By the mid-nineteenth century, however, the value of education was being gauged on a scale of 'method' and 'thoroughness' (Cohen, 2004).

Like its rise in popularity, the demise of the familiar format can be related to the shift in the meaning and function of conversation in the practice of politeness and sociability, and as a corollary, to the shifting value attributed to conversation in children's domestic education. There must be other reasons too, connected to the cataclysmic social and political changes that took place during the period of the format's popularity, but these are beyond the scope of this article. One crucial change needs further exploration: as arguments for the superiority of schooling over home education increased in power, as revealed by the disapproval of domestic education of headmistresses such as Frances Mary Buss and Dorothea Beale in their testimonies to the Schools Inquiry Commission (Report from the Commissioners, 1867–1868), the popularity of the familiar format declined. The historical trajectory of the familiar format can contribute to illuminating how this shift, which involved profound changes in pedagogical theory—not always for the better (Cannon, 1984)—over the course of a century of educational practices, took place.

Disclosure statement

No potential conflict of interest was reported by the author.

HOME EDUCATION IN HISTORICAL PERSPECTIVE

References

A Mother. (1826). *Thoughts on domestic education: the result of experience*. London.
Adeane, J. H. (Ed.). (1896). *The girlhood of Maria Josepha Holroyd (Lady Stanley of Alderley) recorded in letters of a hundred years ago: from 1776 to 1796*. London: Longmans Green and Co.
Aikin, J., & Barbauld, A. L. (1846 [1792–1796]). *Evenings at home*. London: James Cornish.
Allan, D. (2008). *Making British culture: English readers and the Scottish Enlightenment, 1740–1830*. New York: Routledge.
[Allen, C]. (1775). *The polite lady; or A course of female education. In a series of letters* (3rd ed.). London.
Amies, M. (1985). Amusing and instructive conversations: The literary genre and its relevance to home education. *History of Education, 14*(2), 87–99.
Anon. (1823). *The boarding school; or Familiar conversations between a governess and her pupils, written for the amusement and instruction of young ladies*. London: G. & W.B. Whittaker.
Anon. (1831). *Austin Hall; or After dinner conversations between a father and his children, on subjects of amusement and instruction*. London: Baldwin & Cradock.
Arizpe, E., & Styles, M. (2004). 'Love to learn your book': Children's experiences of text in the eighteenth century. *History of Education, 33*(May), 337–352.
Borsay, P. (2006). Children, adolescents and fashionable urban society in eighteenth-century England. In A. Müller (Ed.), *Fashioning childhood in the eighteenth century: Age and identity* (pp. 53–62). Aldershot: Ashgate.
Bryant, M. (1985). The education of girls and women. In J. Purvis (Ed.), *Proceedings of the 1984 annual conference of the history of education society*. London: History of Education Society.
Butler, M. (1972). *Maria Edgeworth, a literary biography*. Oxford: Clarendon Press.
Cannon, J. (1984). *Aristocratic century: The peerage of eighteenth-century England*. Cambridge: Cambridge University Press.
Castalia, Countess Granville (Ed.). (1916). *Private correspondence 1781–1821*. 2 vols. London: John Murray.
Chapone, H. (1775). On conversation, in *Miscellanies in Prose and Verse*. London: C. Dilly.
Clarke, N. (1997). The cursed Barbauld crew: women writers and writing for children in the late eighteenth century. In M. Hilton, M. Styles, & V. Watson (Eds.), *Opening the nursery door: Reading, writing and childhood, 1600–1900* (pp. 91–103). London: Routledge.
Cohen, M. (1996). *Fashioning masculinity: National identity and language in the eighteenth century*. London: Routledge.
Cohen, M. (2004). Gender and the private/public debate on education in the long eighteenth century. In R. Aldrich (Ed.), *Public or private education? Lessons from history* (pp. 15–35). London: Woburn Press.
Cohen, M. (2005a). 'Manners' make the man: Politeness, chivalry, and the construction of masculinity, 1750–1830. *Journal of British Studies, 44*(April), 312–329.
Cohen, M. (2005b). 'To think, to compare, to combine, to methodise': Notes towards rethinking girls' education in the eighteenth century. In S. Knott & B. Taylor (Eds.), *Women, gender and Enlightenment* (pp. 224–242). London: Palgrave.
Cohen, M. (2006). 'A little learning': The curriculum and the construction of gender difference in the long eighteenth century. *British Journal for Eighteenth-Century Studies, 29*, 321–335.
Cohen, M. (2008). 'A proper exercise for the mind': Conversation and education in the long eighteenth century. In K. Halsey & J. Slinn (Eds.), *The concept and practice of conversation in the long eighteenth century* (pp. 98–122). Cambridge: Cambridge Scholars Press.
Cohen, M. (2009). 'Familiar explanations': Social conversations, familiar conversations and domestic education in late eighteenth-century England. In M. Hilton & J. Shefrin (Eds.), *Educating the child in Enlightenment Britain: Beliefs, cultures, practices* (pp. 99–118). Farnham, Surrey: Ashgate.

Cowper, W. (1827). *The letters of the late William Cowper, Esq. to his friends. A new edition*. London: Longman, Rees, Orme, Brown and Green.

Delany, M. (1861). *The autobiography and correspondence of Mary Granville, Mrs Delany*. 1st ser. 3 vols (L. Llanover, Ed.). London: Richard Bentley.

Dille, C. (2013 July). Familiar learning: Sibling educators in fact and fiction. *Paper presented at the Pride and prejudices: Women's writing of the long eighteenth century* conference, Chawton.

Doran, J. (1873). *A lady of the last century (Mrs Elizabeth Montagu)*. London: Richard Bentley and Son.

Edgeworth, M., & Edgeworth, R. L. (1798/1801). *Practical education*. 3 vols. London: J. Johnson.

Eger, E. (2005). 'The noblest commerce of mankind': Conversation and community in the bluestocking circle. In S. Knott & B. Taylor (Eds.), *Women, gender and enlightenment* (pp. 288–305). London: Palgrave.

Fletcher, [E]. (1874). *Autobiography of Mrs. [Eliza] Fletcher, of Edinburgh, with selections from her letters and other family memorials*, compiled and arranged by the survivor of her family. Carlisle.

Forsyth, J. S. (1827). *The first lines of botany or, Primer to the Linnaean system*. London: James Bulcock.

Fyfe, A. (1999). How the squirrel became a squgg: The long history of a children's book. *Paradigm*, no. 27, 25–37. Retrieved from http://faculty.ed.uiuc.edu/westbury/paradigm/fyfe2.html http://hdl.handle.net/10023/5383

Fyfe, A. (2000a). Reading children's books in late eighteenth-century dissenting families. *The Historical Journal*, 43, 453–473.

Fyfe, A. (2000b). Young readers and the sciences. In M. Frasca-Spada & N. Jardine (Eds.), *Books and the sciences in history* (pp. 276–290). Cambridge: Cambridge University Press.

Fyfe, A. (2008). Tracts, classics and brands: Science for children in the nineteenth century. In J. Briggs, D. Butt, & M. Grenby (Eds.), *Popular children's literature in Britain* (pp. 209–228). Aldershot: Ashgate.

Gates, B. T. (1998). *Kindred nature: Victorian and Edwardian women embrace the living world*. London: University of Chicago Press.

Genlis, S-F. Comtesse de. (2007 [1783]). *Adelaide and Theodore, or Letters on education*. (G. Dow, Ed.). London: Pickering and Chatto.

Gleadle, K. (2003). Opinions deliver'd in conversation: Conversation, politics, and gender in the late eighteenth century. In J. Harris (Ed.), *Civil society in British history: Ideas, identities, institutions* (pp. 61–78). Oxford: Oxford University Press.

Grenby, M. O. (2003). Politicizing the nursery: British children's literature and the French revolution. *The Lion and the Unicorn*, 27, 15.

Grenby, M. O. (2009). Delightful instruction? Assessing children's use of educational books in the long eighteenth century. In M. Hilton & J. Shefrin (Eds.), *Educating the child in Enlightenment Britain: Beliefs, cultures, practices* (pp. 181–198). Farnham, Surrey: Ashgate.

Grenby, M. O. (2011). *The child reader 1700–1840*. Cambridge: Cambridge University Press.

Hannan, L. (2013). Women, letter-writing and the life of the mind in England, c.1650–1750. *Literature & History*, 22(2), 1–19.

Helme, E. (1804). *The history of Scotland related in familiar conversations by a father to his children: Interspersed with moral and instructive remarks, and observations on the most leading and interesting subjects, designed for the perusal of youth*. London: Longman, Hurst Rees, and Orme.

Higginson, Mrs A. (1859). *The English schoolgirl: Her position and duties, in a series of lessons form a teacher to her class*. London: Chapman and Hall.

Hilton, M. (2007). *Women and the shaping of the nation's young: Education and public doctrine in Britain 1750–1850*. Aldershot, Hampshire: Ashgate.

Hilton, M., & Shefrin, J. (Eds.). (2009). *Educating the child in Enlightenment Britain: Beliefs, cultures, practices*. Farnham, Surrey: Ashgate.

Hymes, D. (1972). Models of the interaction of language and social life. In J. Gumperz & D. Hymes (Eds.), *Directions in sociolinguistics: The ethnography of communication* (pp. 35–71). New York: Holt, Rinehart, Winston.

Jamieson, A. (1819). *Conversations on general history: Exhibiting a progressive view of the state of mankind, from the earliest ages of which we have any authentic records, to the beginning of the year 1819.* London: G. and W. B. Whittaker.

Keene, M. (2014). Familiar science in nineteenth-century Britain. *HS, 52*(1), 53–71.

Klein, L. E. (1994). *Shaftesbury and the culture of politeness: Moral discourse and cultural politics in early eighteenth-century England.* Cambridge: Cambridge University Press.

Larpent, A. HL HM. 31201 *Mrs Larpent's Diary* m.1016 -1-7.

Macaulay, C. (1790). *Letters on education; with observations on religious and metaphysical subjects.* Dublin.

Marcet, J. (1806). *Conversations on chemistry, in which the elements of that science are familiarly explained.* 2 vols. London: Longman, Hurst, Rees, & Orme.

Marcet, J. (1842). *Conversations on the history of England for the use of children.* London: Longman, Brown, Green and Longmans.

Markham Mrs [pseud Elizabeth Penrose]. (1823). *History of England for the use of young persons.* London.

Mee, J. (2011). *Conversable worlds: Literature, contention, and community 1762 to 1830.* Oxford: Oxford University Press.

Mercer, N., & Littleton, K. (2007). *Dialogue and the development of children's thinking: A sociocultural approach.* London: Routledge.

Meredith, N. (1810). *Rudiments of chemical philosophy; in which the first principles of that useful and entertaining science are familiarly explained and illustrated.* London.

Murry, A. (1778). *Mentoria, or the young ladies instructor; in familiar conversations on moral and entertaining subjects, etc.* London.

Myers, G. (1989). Science for women and children: The dialogue of popular science in the nineteenth century. In J. Christie & S. Shuttleworth (Eds.), *Nature transfigured: Science and literature.* Manchester: Manchester University Press (pp. 171–209).

Myers, G. (1997). Fictionality, demonstration, and a forum for popular science: Jane Marcet's *Conversation on chemistry*. In B. T. Gates & A. B. Shteir (Eds.), *Natural eloquence: Women reinscribe science* (pp. 43–60). London: University of Wisconsin Press.

Myers, M. (1986). Impeccable governesses, rational dames, and moral mothers: Mary Wollstonecraft and the female tradition in Georgian children's books. *Children's Literature, 14*, 31–59.

Parry, G. (2007). Education and the reproduction of the Enlightenment. In M. Fitzpatrick et al. (Eds.), *The Enlightenment world* (pp. 217–233). London: Routledge.

Pearson, J. (1999). *Women's reading in Britain 1750–1835: A dangerous recreation.* Cambridge: Cambridge University Press.

Pujol, S. (2005). *Le dialogue d'idées au dix-huitième siècle.* Oxford: Voltaire Foundation.

Report from the Commissioners. (1867–1868). *Schools inquiry commission (Taunton Commission).* 20 vols. London: HMSO.

Rippingham, J. (1815). *Natural history; according to the Linnaean system, explained by familiar dialogues in visits to the London Museum.* 4 vols. London: John Sharpe.

Robertson, J. (1798). *An essay on the education of young ladies.* London: T. Cadell.

Robinson, M. (1930 [1801]). *Memoirs of the late Mrs Robinson, written by herself.* London.

Rogers, B. (1958). *Georgian chronicle: Mrs Barbauld and her family.* London: Methuen and Co.

Secord, J. (1985). Newton in the nursery: Tom Telescope and the philosophy of tops and balls, 1761–1838. *History of Science, xxiii*, 127–151.

Secord, J. (2007). How scientific conversation became shop talk. In A. Fyfe & B. Lightman (Eds.), *Science in the marketplace* (pp. 23–59). Chicago, IL: University of Chicago Press.

Shore, E. (1891). *The journal of Emily Shore*. London: Kegan Paul, Trench, Trübner.
Shteir, A. (1996). *Cultivating women, cultivating science: Flora's daughters and botany in England*. Baltimore & London: Johns Hopkins University Press.
Skedd, S. (1997). Women teachers and the expansion of girls' schooling in England, c1760–1820. In H. Barker & E. Chalus (Eds.), *Gender in eighteenth-century England: Roles, representations and responsibilities* (pp. 101–25). Harlow: Longman.
Stray, C. (1998). *Classics transformed: Schools, universities, and society in England, 1830–1960*. Oxford: Clarendon Press.
Sutherland, K. (2000). Writings on education and conduct: arguments for female improvement. In V. Jones (Ed.), *Women and literature in Britain, 1700-1800* (pp. 25–45). Cambridge: Cambridge University Press.
Tague, I. (2002). *Women of quality: Accepting and contesting ideals of femininity in England, 1690–1760*. Woodbridge: Boydell.
Wakefield, P. (1794). *Mental improvement*. 2 vols. London: Darton and Harvey.
Walters, A. N. (1997). Conversation pieces: Science and politeness in eighteenth-century England. *History of Science, xxxv*, 121–154.
Wollstonecraft, M. (1788). *Original stories from real life*. London: J. Johnson.
Wright, J. H. (1840). *Breakfast table science: Written expressly for the amusement and instruction of young people*. London: Thomas Tegg.

Children's literature, the home, and the debate on public versus private education, c.1760–1845

M. O. Grenby
Newcastle University, UK

In Britain in the period 1760–1845 the debate on the relative merits of public (school) versus private (home) education remained unresolved and was vigorously debated in many media. It was in this same period that children's literature began to flourish: a much wider variety of books were published in much greater numbers. The new children's literature generally took domestic life for its subject; its authors often claimed that their books had emerged from domestic practice; and the books were often marketed as being for domestic use. It can seem, therefore, that the new children's literature was, in essence, a materialisation in print of domestic pedagogy, a product developed to supply a growing demand for didactic materials to use in the home. This essay will test the hypothesis, considering some real-life pedagogical practices and examining a wide range of later eighteenth- and early nineteenth-century children's texts (both print and manuscript). This evidence will show in fact that the boundaries between private and public education were blurred. Moreover, some children's books were themselves interventions into the debate on private versus public schooling. They presented a utopian, if still practical, vision of how the advantages of both models could be combined.

In 1806, the painter Joseph Farington praised in his diary Jane Harley, Countess of Oxford, for showing 'the greatest attention to the education of Her children', being 'constantly with them from ten oClock in the morning till one, during which time they receive instructions'. Particularly commended was that she directly supervised their reading, 'never allow[ing] a book of any kind except such as she may have read and approved, to lay in a room to which the Children have access' (Farington, 1924, vol. 4, p. 31). Farington may have been surprised at this, for Lady Harley was by no means regarded as a paragon of domesticity (indeed, the reverse).

Certainly it was no idle observation. Rather it was Farington's private reflection on a debate raging in the late eighteenth and early nineteenth century on the virtues of private versus public education. Diaries, journals and letters are full of individual opinions on the topic. School prospectuses and lengthy treatises give the views of teachers and theorists. Parents expressed their preferences in the schooling choices they made. Novelists, and children's novelists in particular, discussed the issue as a perennially unsettled question. As late as 1874, Henry William Pullen could fill almost half of his *The Ground Ash: A Public School Story* with a debate between a squire and a rector on the relative merits of domestic versus public school education. 'Innumerable', wrote the philosopher William Godwin in 1797, 'are the discussions that have originated in the comparative advantages of public and private education' (Godwin, 1797, p. 56). He then proceeded to set out his own ideas on the question.

The relative merits that people assigned to home and school education were dependent on many factors: the age, gender, class and religion of the children in question, as well as where in Britain they lived and the different types of schooling available. Michèle Cohen contends that, by the end of the eighteenth century, public education 'became associated with masculinity, and "private" with femininity and effeminacy' (Cohen, 2004, p. 29). But if, as a whole, domestic and school pedagogies were increasingly differentiated by gender, the debate, in its detail, resists attempts to impose on it a single, simple trajectory. Individuals were certainly still advocating public education for middle- and upper-class girls at the end of the eighteenth century and after: Erasmus Darwin, for instance, whose *Plan for the Conduct of Female Education, in Boarding Schools* (1797) was emphatic about the superiority of school to domestic education, and later Frances Broadhurst's 'A Word in Favour of Female Schools' (1827) and Harriet Martineau's *Household Education* (1849). Indeed, the number of commercially-run girls' schools in the years around 1800 (many of them run by women) seems to have increased rather than declined (Skedd, 1997). Equally, domestic education for boys continued to be widely advocated right across the period. When the Rev. John Bennett amassed his many arguments demonstrating that 'a *mother* should be the *preceptress* of her children', he made no distinction between boys' and girls' education (Bennett, 1787, pp. 151–152). In many cases, a father's domestic education of his sons was evidently a matter of great pride. In his *Autobiography*, for example, John Stuart Mill (born 1806) recalled that his father employed 'a considerable part of almost every day ... in the instruction of his [nine] children', exerting 'an amount of labour, care, and perseverance rarely, if ever, employed for a similar purpose, in endeavouring to give, according to his own conception, the highest order of intellectual education'. It was an education that encompassed Latin, Greek (beginning when Mill was three) and history (tested on daily father-and-son walks in the lanes around their home), while arithmetic 'was the task of the evenings' (Mill, 1981, vol. 1, pp. 7–12). Evidently, domestic education might be no less rigorous, extensive or demanding than what was provided by schools.

HOME EDUCATION IN HISTORICAL PERSPECTIVE

In short, in the period 1760–1845, although the landscape of educational provision changed significantly, the debate over the advantages of domestic or institutional pedagogy remained unsettled and among the middle classes and the elites 'private' or home education was by no means in retreat. Indeed, whether for boys or girls, what we now call 'home-schooling' was often upheld as optimal. Moreover, as Sophia Woodley has shown, the choice of private or public education was seldom a matter of indifference or merely a question of practicality. Rather, parents' decisions were generally informed, the result of sustained engagement with works of educational philosophy, or ideological, made on the basis of religious creed or political convictions (Woodley, 2009).

What this essay will explore is the links between domestic education and the children's literature of the period. Young people had been reading before the later eighteenth century of course, but the number and range of books published specifically for them in Britain expanded markedly from the 1740s, and exponentially from the 1780s. At first sight, many of these books seem to be focussed on the domestic. Whether moral tales or travel writing, fairy stories or conduct literature, poetry or instructional works, publishers and authors presented children's books as having derived from the home and as fit to be used there. The book titles themselves repeatedly enforce this point: John Aikin and Anna Laetitia Barbauld's *Evenings at Home* (1792–1796); *The Happy Family at Eason House, Exhibited in the Amiable Conduct of the Little Nelsons and Their Parents* (1799); *Domestic Pleasures; or, the Happy Fire-Side* (1816) by Frances Bowyer Vaux. So too do advertisements and illustrations, and the many authorial prefaces that diffidently explain how the text that follows had been written for use in the author's family and published only with reluctance. Given the public debate around domestic education, it is tempting to speculate that this new children's literature emerged to fill a need for books to use in educational schemes in household settings. Certainly, the children's author and critic Sarah Trimmer seemed to acknowledge this in 1782, enthusing that 'those parents who chuse to educate their own children, may meet with a variety of books to assist them in the pleasing task' (Trimmer, 1782–1785, preface). It is the validity of this hypothesis that the essay will investigate. Was the new children's literature conceived and promoted for use in the home? Was it an intervention in the debate on private versus public education, specifically endorsing the former? Was the new children's literature, in short, the printed manifestation of domestic pedagogy?

1. Children's literature and domesticity

From its inception, the implied users of the new children's literature were parents, not teachers, who were encouraged to use the books in the home, not the school. *A Little Pretty Pocket-Book* (c. 1744), published by John Newbery and one of the very earliest of the new children's books, exhibits this clearly. Its dedication is 'To the parents, guardians, and nurses, in Great-Britain and Ireland', and the introduction urges mothers and fathers, not tutors or teachers, to play an active part in their children's education (Anon, 1760, pp. 4, 7–8).

Over the next decades the association between children's literature and domestic education became entrenched, particularly as publishers like the Newberys ceded their position as the innovators of children's literature to the 'Impeccable Governesses, Rational Dames, and Moral Mothers' who, Mitzi Myers has shown, 'found in children's books not just an outlet available to their sex, but a genuine vocation' (Myers, 1986, p. 33). In the debate on public versus private education, these authors can seem strongly to have favoured the latter. Sarah Trimmer, for instance, children's author and the first serious critic of children's literature, educated her six sons and six daughters at home (only sending the boys to a local clergyman for tuition in classical languages). The children's books she published from 1780 with much trepidation were written for her children and were, she said, attempts to supply a need that her domestic pedagogy had identified (1780, p. viii; 1786, pp. ix–x). Regardless of politics and denomination, the same concerns and hopes activated other pioneering and popular children's writers, including Lady Ellenor Fenn, Anna Laetitia Barbauld, Mary Wollstonecraft and Maria Edgeworth. Edgeworth for instance, after unhappy experiences of her own when sent away to school, educated her 13 younger half-siblings at home, experimenting with new pedagogical techniques and documenting their progress. She was careful to explain that the principles she set out in the treatise *Practical Education* (published under her own and her father's name in 1798) applied to both public and private pedagogy. But when considering children's literature she announced that her thoughts chiefly concerned 'children who are to be brought up in a private family' (Edgeworth & Edgeworth, 1798, vol. 1, p. 324). Notably, she praised Barbauld's *Lessons for Children* (1778–1779) for its homeliness: 'Mrs Barbauld has judiciously chosen to introduce a little boy's daily history in these books' which will make 'all children … extremely interested' because 'they are very apt to expect that every thing which happens to him [the book's protagonist] is to happen to them' (Edgeworth & Edgeworth, 1798, vol. 1, pp. 318–319). Edgeworth's own writing for children, beginning in 1796 with *The Parent's Assistant*, naturally followed suit.

Fenn, in her *Rational Sports, In Dialogues Passing Among the Children of a Family* (1783a) claimed that 'It is the father's province to attend to the school education; I design to treat of that which belongs to the mother' (Fenn, 1783a, p. xi). But in fact domestic education did not belong exclusively to mothers, for many of the men who wrote for children in the later eighteenth century also claimed that their work had begun in a programme of domestic education. Thomas Day, for instance, begins his *Sandford and Merton* by noting that 'All, who have been conversant in the education of very young children, have complained of the total want to proper books to be put into their hands, while they are taught the elements of reading', insisting 'I have felt this want in common with others, and have been very much embarrassed how to supply it' (Day, 1783–1789, vol. 1, pp. iii–iv). The bestselling *Sandford and Merton* was his solution. It is a novel which vilifies the education on offer at any 'public school', at which 'every vice and folly … is commonly taught', and which the squirearchy are shown to prefer merely because they allow boys to 'make genteel connections' (Day, 1783–1789, vol. 2, pp. 241, 234). Day recommended instead a thoroughly independent and egalitarian pedagogy, provided in homes and gardens by the local clergyman Mr Barlow to his two eponymous heroes, one rich, the other poor.

Overall it is clear, then, that the new children's literature, whether schoolbook or pleasure-reading, was presented as having emerged from actual domestic practice. John Ash, for example, tells us that he only ventured to publish his celebrated and long-lasting *Grammatical Institutes: or Grammar, Adapted to the Genius of the English Tongue* (1760), because of his success in using it with his five-year-old daughter (Navest, 2011, p. 29). John Carey (dubbed a 'Classical Teacher' on his title-page) maintained that his *Learning Better than House and Land* (1808) was 'not originally written with a view to publication, but solely intended for the amusement and instruction of an amiable and interesting youth, a private pupil of mine' (Carey, n.d. [1808], p. i). Many of Fenn's prefaces give precise details about how the books she made at home for her nieces' and nephews' use came to be published (see Delaney, 2012, p. 58ff). As Edgeworth put it in *The Parent's Assistant* (1796): 'It seems a very easy task to write for children' but 'Those only who have been interested in the education of a family … can feel the dangers and difficulties of such an undertaking' (Edgeworth, 1796, p. iv).[1]

Second, the new children's literature was being presented not simply as something for children to read, but as a tool for home-schooling parents. Explicit in setting this out is the sub-title of Fenn's *Rational Sports* (c.1783) which explains that the book is 'Designed as a hint to mothers how they may inform the minds of their little people Respecting The Objects With Which They Are Surrounded'. Wollstonecraft's translation of Christian Gotthilf Salzmann's *Elements of Morality* (1790) took this further, prefacing the narrative itself with an 'Introductory Address to Parents'. 'I now present this book to you', writes the author, 'earnestly wishing that it may have a proper effect on your children … But I must say a few words to you concerning the right use of it' (Salzmann, 1790, vol. 1, p. xiii). What follows is a set of lessons in the proprieties of book use: do not let children read the book themselves but read it to them in short bursts, sometimes breaking off suddenly; read it 'after dinner, during a walk, or when the children themselves beg you to tell them something'; assume the voice and manner of the personages in the story; draw attention to the illustrations; fit the extract being read to the present behaviour of the child; question the children on what they have heard (vol. 1, pp. xiv–xvii). Similarly, speaking of 'books of science and general knowledge', Maria Budden advised mothers 'to read the book herself, and give her children the information it contains in her own words' (Budden, 1826, pp. 33–34). The same principles applied even to fiction, and many children's novels begin with frontispieces that clearly show the book in the hands of a parent to whom children raptly attend. Such modes of use were the norm, at least in terms of prescription if not actual practice (Grenby, 2011, pp. 242–247). They applied not only to very young children, nor only to boys.

Third, if the new children's literature was *of* and *for* the domestic household, it was also almost always *about* the home. This familial *mise-en-scène* was frequently recorded even in book titles, and authors of the new children's literature made a virtue of the smallness of their canvases. As the preface to the English translation of Arnaud Berquin's *L'Ami des enfans* (1782 [translated version 1786]) put it, contrasting the new children's literature with what had gone before, 'Instead of those wild fictions of the Wonderful, in which their understanding is too commonly bewilder'd, they [child readers] will here see only what occurs or may occur within the limits of their families'. Children reading his book, Berquin continued, would be 'accompanied by none, except their parents, the companions of their pastimes' (Berquin, 1786, vol. 1, pp. 16–17). Texts that might have opened up the world to children were methodically constricted. Thus in *The New Robinson Crusoe* (a 1788 translation of Joachim Heinrich Campe's *Robinson der Jüngere*) the story of Defoe's adventurous and independent castaway was re-framed as an account given to his children, his wife and occasional visiting friends by Mr Billingsley, an archetypal educating father, around the parlour fire over a series of 31 evenings. The children write letters to Crusoe (one wonders how the original Crusoe, notorious for filial disobedience, would have received their advice to 'Take pains to be industrious and good' for 'that will please every body, and especially your father and mother' (Campe, 1788, vol. 2, p. 22)). But the furthest away from home they get is a field trip to Margate. What Myers calls 'domestic realism' was the prevailing form of the new children's literature: 'colloquial dialogues and conversations, homely natural and household detail, anecdotes of meaningful moral choice drawn from the everyday world' (Myers, 1986, p. 38).

Indeed, in the majority of children's moral tales the outside world was presented as a dangerous place. The world was full of swindlers and assailants, rivers in which one might drown and 'gipseys' plotting abduction. The furthest from home that most fictional children were allowed to go without mishap was the garden, and children's fictions were frequently set in arbours, bowers or summer houses, a 'transitional zone', as Elise L. Smith notes, 'set apart from the wildness of nature but more flexible, both spatially and socially, than the confined rooms of the home', and where adult observation could unobtrusively continue (Smith, 2008, pp. 45, 24). In particular, although the new children's literature did include school stories, school was presented as full of perils. In Edgeworth's 'The Barring-Out; or, Party Spirit' (1796) the school is riven by factions and the boys become progressively more depraved, finally seizing control of their classroom and shutting out their teacher. In George Walker's *The Adventures of Timothy Thoughtless: or, the Misfortunes of a Little Boy who ran away from Boarding-School* (1813), 10-year-old Timothy, having been sent away to Greengrove House school in Northamptonshire, falls in with his 'evil-disposed' schoolfellow Will Grumble, who persuades him to run away rather than face the school's harsh discipline. Following their escape, Grumble dies and Thoughtless is robbed, becomes a beggar, poorhouse inmate, and chimney-sweep, before being tearfully reunited with his family. Indeed, school was a watchword for vice. In Trimmer's *Fabulous Histories* (1786), written to encourage children 'to shew compassion to the *Animal Creation*', the children are divided neatly into two groups, those who are home-schooled who are kind to animals, and those sent to school, who are not (Trimmer, 1786, p. vii). Selfish, even callous parents, send their children to schools, like Trimmer's Mrs Addis who, too fond of animals, lavishes all her love on her pets, and remarks 'I am obliged to keep the boy [her son] almost continually at school, for he is so cruel to my *dear little precious creatures*, that there is no bearing him *at home*' (p. 102). Or school can be a punishment, as in Lucy Watkins' *The History and Adventures of Little James and Mary* (1813), where, because she is 'obstinate and sullen' at home, Mary's parents hope that 'a poor parish school ... will teach her industry'. The humbling experience works, and her mother welcomes her back. 'Pleased to hear she is to stay at home, she resolves not to neglect her book' (Watkins, 1813, p. 27).

In fact, one might argue that the whole genre of the school story, emerging around the turn of the nineteenth century, was founded not on enthusiasm for public schooling but on scepticism. Dorothy Kilner's *Anecdotes of a Boarding-School* (*c*.1790) conceded that schooling outside the home could sometimes be necessary ('Were your mamma's time at her own disposal, I doubt not but she would gladly dedicate every moment to your improvement; and, by her assiduity, amply supply the place of all other instructions'), but the 'attendant evils ... which await a boarding-school education, are such, as ... counter-balance the advantages that arise from it'. Kilner explains that she wrote the book, one of the earliest school stories, as (oxymoronically) 'an Antidote to the *vices* of those *useful* seminaries' (Kilner, *c*.1790, vol. 1, pp. vi–vi; emphasis added). A domestic education, on the other hand, was the ideal, as practised, for instance, by Mr Billingsley in *The New Robinson Crusoe*:

> having a pretty large family, and but a moderate fortune, [he] determined to undertake himself the care of his children's education. He proposed, by this plan, on the one hand, to avoid the enormous expence of keeping them at what are called genteel boarding-schools, and, on the other, to enjoy the pleasing observation of their improvement in learning, sense, and good behaviour. To remark, with silent but attentive eyes, the gradual advance of his children towards the perfection of reason and virtue; to assist, with his advice and instruction, their endeavours to become more learned, honest, and wise; and to have the happy consciousness, that he should one day be considered, what all parents ought, as the instrument and cause of his children's eternal welfare; all this, he thought, would be more than sufficient reward for whatever cares and fatigue he should undergo in the course of their education. (Campe, 1788, pp. 23–24)

The logic of Mr Billingsley's educational decision, and its sentimental appeal, was designed to be difficult to resist.

Likewise, Edgeworth's 'The Good Aunt' (from *Moral Tales*, 1801 in Edgeworth, 2013) offers a dramatised intervention into the debate on public and private education. The eponymous aunt had systematically 'educated herself, that she might be able to fulfil the important duty of educating a child' (Edgeworth, 2013, p. 100). Her instruction of her orphaned nephew, Charles, is exemplary, and notably domestic, not only in that it happens at home, but also because her tools of instruction are both books and 'The conversation of the sensible, well-informed people who visited Mrs. Howard', for 'A child may learn as much from conversation as from books; not so many historic facts, but as much instruction' (p. 101). Only the Latin and Greek is outsourced, to a private tutor. However, when Charles is 'about thirteen' (p. 107) his aunt loses her wealth and she is forced to send Charles to Westminster School, she herself setting up a boarding house there for a number of pupils. In contrast to the serene and enlightened learning environment of Mrs Howard's home, the school is a brutal and deeply unscholarly place, where snobbishness and bullying are endemic. Edgeworth's preference seems clear. To favour public education would be to align oneself with the foolish Mrs Holloway, one of Mrs Howard's visitors, who bases her preference for public schooling on the experience of her son Augustus (one of the school's worst bullies as it turns out). She boasts of Augustus' proficiency in Latin but adds (condemning herself out of her own mouth) 'to be sure, it was flogged into him well at first, at a public school, which, I understand, is the best way of making good scholars' (p. 105).

We will return to Mrs Holloway, an imprudent and unsympathetic mother who, like Trimmer's Mrs Addis, sends her son away to school because she is unwilling to curtail her own pleasures by educating him herself. For now, though, we should note that Edgeworth's apparent repugnance to public schooling fits into a larger picture. The prevailing view on education adopted by the new children's literature seems set: the parent is the proper teacher, the home the proper schoolroom, and (unless warning against the dangers of leaving it) the household the proper subject for a children's book. These initial conclusions, however, need to be subjected to further scrutiny.

2. Continuity not dichotomy

We should be cautious about reading the new children's literature purely as a product developed for the domestic market or as a textual manifestation of arguments being made in favour of domestic education.

First, the line between home and school education was often very blurred. Public schooling, particularly in rural areas, was often extremely informal, sourced on an *ad hoc* and intermittent basis to supplement, not replace, home-schooling. 'Groups of parents ... banded together to find teachers for their children', Susan Whyman concludes from her reading of family letters, hiring 'local residents, often women, who charged by the week and might be paid with local produce' who would set up school in 'makeshift places of instruction' like 'parlours and porches' that 'do not appear in lists of licensed schools' (Whyman, 2009, pp. 87, 107). The small schools that began to proliferate in the late eighteenth century, especially for girls, also 'often fall into a gap between formal definitions of public and private education' because they were often established by a single 'master' or 'governess', lasted only until that single teacher retired, and often 'advertised themselves as offering a familial, affectionate and *domestic* environment' (Hilton & Shefrin, 2009, pp. 10–11). Even at the major boys' boarding schools the line between public and private education could be indistinct, the pupils generally living in 'houses' (like that established by Edgeworth's Good Aunt) and almost always having their classroom instruction supplemented by private tuition. Further, parental supervision often did not diminish for those away at boarding schools. As Whyman and Clare Brant both note, letters flowed between parents and children, often providing quite formal instruction alongside the general advice and family news, and, argues Brant, acting as a tool of surveillance (Brant, 2006, pp. 65, 76–77; Whyman, 2009, pp. 37–41). In Fenn's early school story *School Occurrences*, Miss Worthy's mother establishes an outpost of home in the potentially hostile territory of school by annotating her daughter's books to show her which passages she may read and which she may not. Miss Pert, a schoolfellow, is scornful: 'I wonder that you have not strings to your eye-lids, and the ends kept in your Mamma's hands' (Fenn, 1783b, pp. 88–94). Those strings are supposed to show that home and school need not be, nor should not be, entirely separate worlds.

Moreover, the debate on public versus private education was not always as polarised as we might imagine. Edgeworth's starting position in *Practical Education* was that 'A father, who has time, talents, and temper, to educate his family, is certainly the best possibly preceptor, and his rewards will be the highest degree of domestic facility'. Yet when pushed to confront the realities of middle-class childcare in the late eighteenth century, Edgeworth acknowledged that such an ideal education would not always be possible, for 'how are men in business or in trade, artists or manufacturers, to educate their families, when they have not time to attend to them' or 'may not think themselves perfectly prepared to undertake the classical instruction, and entire education of boys'? (Edgeworth & Edgeworth, 1798, vol. 2, p. 502). Her solution (for boys, implicitly) was therefore a continuum that mixed public and private: 'In his father's house the first important lessons, those which decide his future abilities and character, must be learned', she wrote, recommending a system in which 'parents educated their children well for the first eight or nine years of their lives, and then sent them all to public seminaries' (vol. 2, p. 505). Naturally, *Moral Tales*, the volume of stories 'written to illustrate the opinions delivered in *Practical Education*' (and in which 'The Good Aunt' appeared), supported this opinion. In its preface, Richard Lovell Edgeworth conceded that public schools can form character and develop potential, but argues that the 'solid advantages' of school education must be 'secured by previous domestic instruction' (Edgeworth, 2003, vol. 10, p. 170). In this light, the apparent critiques of public schooling presented in Edgeworth's and Trimmer's children's fiction become less attacks on public schooling *per se* than on inadequate parenthood (especially motherhood) as embodied by Mrs Holloway and Mrs Addis. It is these parents' failure to prepare their sons for school that leads to the children's scholastic shortcomings and moral collapse once there—their bullying and cruelty—not the institutions themselves.

If Edgeworth's writing on education proposed a pragmatic supersession model that linked private and public pedagogy sequentially, others thought that home and school should be thoroughly interfused. In his 1797 essay discussing 'Public and Private Education', Godwin concluded that 'The objections to both the modes of education here discussed are of great magnitude' so that 'It is unavoidable to enquire, whether a middle way might not be selected, neither entirely public, or entirely private, avoiding the mischiefs of each, and embracing the advantages of both' (Godwin, 1797, p. 64). Wollstonecraft had written against public schooling ('hot-beds of vice and folly') but in *A Vindication of the Rights of Woman* she wrote that 'further experience has led me to view the subject in a different light' and she worried that schooling at home meant that children 'there acquire too high an opinion of their own importance' (Wollstonecraft, 1792, pp. 363–364). Children learn best, she concluded, among other children, and her solution, as Alan Richardson summarises, was to call for 'a middle ground between the inadequate pedagogy and supervision of boarding-schools and the confinement of an adult-dominated "private" education ... where children can learn together while enjoying the domestic comforts—and maintaining the domestic ties—of home' (Richardson, 2002, p. 34). Interestingly, Thomas Arnold, the celebrated headmaster of Rugby School from 1827 and of course the inspiration for 'the Doctor' in Thomas Hughes' *Tom Brown's School Days* (1857), thought very similarly. He deplored 'the effect of the public schools of England to lower and weaken the connexion between parent and child', and strongly recommended that boys continue to live at home while attending his school, 'being at once at school and at home'. Thus they would have all the advantages of a professional education and the company of their peers but would also be 'keeping up all their home affections' and 'never losing that lively interest in all that is said and done under their father's roof' (Arnold, 1833, pp. 93 and 96).

The home in which, following Wollstonecraft's death, Godwin brought up five children (two of whom were Wollstonecraft's daughters, three of whom were the children of his second wife, Mary Jane Clairmont) was a real-life example of the 'middle ground' between public and private that Wollstonecraft had sought. As if following Edgeworth's advice about the continuum of education, having educated them at home initially, Godwin sent his two boys to the Charterhouse school as day boys, Charles probably in 1806 aged 11, and his half-brother William in 1811 aged eight. The girls too enjoyed a hybrid private–public education: biographers have recovered a patchwork of paternal tuition, visiting tutors, dame schools and boarding schools. But what is more striking is that the Godwin's private household itself functioned as a semi-public schoolroom, what Julie Carlson characterises as 'a public house or coffeehouse where ideas are read, discussed, composed, diffused', and where children were active participants (Carlson, 2007, p. 82). The diary that Godwin fastidiously kept makes clear that many visitors crossed his threshold, took tea or stayed to supper, or simply joined in the family's educational practices. One such caller, when he was in London from 1808, was Aaron Burr (formerly Thomas Jefferson's vice-president). His journal records that he socialised and engaged in educational activities not only with Godwin himself but with the whole family. He gives some wonderful vignettes of the conduct, and effects, of this private–public education, as for instance in his entry for 15 February 1812:

> In the evening, William, the only son of W. Godwin, a lad of about 9 years old, gave his weekly lecture; having heard how Coleridge and others lectured, he would also lecture;

> and one of his sisters (Mary, I think) writes a lecture, which he reads from a little pulpit which they have erected for him. He went through it with great gravity and decorum. The subject was, 'The Influence of Governments on the Character of the People.' After the lecture we had tea, and the girls sang and danced an hour …. (Burr, 1838, vol. 2, p. 307)

This was an echo of Godwin's memories of his own childhood sermonising: 'in the kitchen every Sunday afternoon, and at other times, mounted in a child's high chair, indifferent as to the number of persons present at my exhibitions, and undisturbed at their coming and going' (Godwin, 1992, p. 17). Godwin understood 'family', Carlson says, 'as a public-oriented relation' and 'home as a sphere of enquiry among familiars', and 'no one at home, not even the children, [was to] be treated as a child or be allowed to act like one' (Carlson, 2007, pp. 84, 86).

The new children's literature could represent exactly this kind of public, pedagogical family. The best known example is probably John Aikin and Anna Lætitia Barbauld's successful *Evenings at Home* (1809 [1792–1796]), set in the exemplary Fairborne household: 'The house was seldom unprovided with visitors … intimate friends or relations of the owners, who were entertained with cheerfulness and hospitality, free from ceremony and parade'. These visitors make an active contribution to the education of the 'numerous progeny of children of both sexes' by writing the short texts that are read on the eponymous evenings to the assembled company, and which fill the six volumes. What is notable is that these reading and discussion sessions take place only when 'all the children were assembled in the holidays', both those 'sent out to school' and those 'educated at home under their parents' care' (Aikin & Barbauld, 1809 [1792–1796], vol. 1, pp. 1–2). 'Evenings at home' are in addition to 'days at school', not an alternative.

In fact, it is probably truer to say that the new children's literature served a hybrid private–public educational model than it did domestic education alone. Titles and paratexts are often careful to stress that no divide existed (perhaps to maximise their market). *A Present for Children*, a miscellany containing catechisms, dialogues, songs, prayers, riddles and fables published in Edinburgh in 1761, was, according to its full title, 'For the use of children, either at home, or at school'. William Butler hoped that his *Geographical and Biographical Exercises, Designed for the Use of Young Ladies* (1799) would add to a growing collection of books 'which have made their way into almost every school and private family' (Butler, 1799, p. v). *Easter Holidays, or Domestic Conversations* (1797), by Althea Fanshawe, builds a bridge between home from school in its very title, and then presents an idealised portrait of the pedagogic mother whose 'eldest son was at a public school' while the instruction of her younger, 'scarcely seven years old', was her 'constant occupation' and 'the most interesting undertaking' (p. 2). She teaches French and Italian to her daughters too, employing masters for their other lessons, although (apparently being in agreement with Wollstonecraft's contention that children learn best among other children) 'by the Masters coming regularly together on the same day, and meeting several more of the neighbours children … they enjoyed the advantages of emulation, and all learned better then [*sic*] could have been the case had each had her lesson singly' (Fanshawe, 1797, p. 2).

Even as the school story became a mature genre in the mid-nineteenth century, it continued to make a case for a blended public–private education in which parents, peers and teachers all contribute to a successful education. A classic example is Harriet Martineau's *The Crofton Boys* (1841). The hero, Hugh, longs to be sent to the boarding school his older brother attends and, finding that the preparatory education he is receiving at home is not profiting him, his parents concede. Initially, he finds the school harsh. He is told that 'To prosper at Crofton, you must put off home' (Martineau, 1841, p. 164). Home and school seem at this stage to be presented as opposites and, as in Hughes' *Tom Brown's School Days*, it is as if the self that had been created at home must be systemically deconstructed so that he can be renewed in the image of the school. Gradually Hugh begins to fit in and prosper, but a boisterous game causes an accident which leads to the amputation of his foot. He returns home where he is nursed back to health by his family. The novel has been described as 'a tale of home values triumphing over school' (Holt, 2008, p. 42) and as containing 'a covert rhetoric of domesticity' (Gargano, 2007, p. 107). But, as Judy Bainbridge argues, it is the joint influence of home and school that enables him to heal: his mother's care but also his schoolmates' determination that he should not wallow in self-pity or become unduly dependent on his family (Bainbridge, 2015, p. 74). Ultimately, he is able to integrate the values and virtues of home *and* school. Strikingly, his mother even connives in the schoolboy code of honour that precludes him from revealing the identity of the boy who had caused his accident, giving a further demonstration of Martineau's conviction that the ethos of the home and the school need not be in competition. Other early Victorian school stories make the same kind of intervention in the debate on public and private education, showing how the two practices might be reconciled: Elizabeth Missing Sewell's *Laneton Parsonage* (1846–1848), for example, and Emily May's *Louis' Schooldays* (1851) (Bainbridge, 2015, pp. 60 and 78–85).

The limited evidence we have of actual practice also suggests that the new children's literature was used in both school and home environments. A copy of Elizabeth Semple's moral tales *Gertrude, Agnes and Melite, and Amelia Douglas* (1804) bears inscriptions giving both a home and a school address. A highly-coloured harlequinade (an early variety of moveable book) entitled *Mother Goose* (1809) is inscribed with a boy's name and where he could be found: '5th Class, / No. 15 Third Desk'. A copy of *Midsummer Holydays* (1790) was apparently taken from home to school, since it was inscribed with the reminder 'to be brought home at Xmas' (Grenby, 2011, p. 205). Books owned by schools seem to have travelled in the other direction too, judging by a printed label pasted into a copy held in the Cotsen Children's Library of John Huddlestone Wynne's *Choice Emblems, Natural, Historical, Fabulous, Moral, and Divine ... For the Use of Schools* (1784). The label identifies the book as the property of 'Ware-School', gives the date 'Christmas, 1785' and records 'This was delivered, whole, neat, covered, and named, to ——', with a blank space for a name to be inserted, and then the note 'N.B. Every injury done to this book is to be laid before Mr. French' (Wynne, 1784). Jan Fergus' revealing work on the number of Newbery books bought by the boys attending Rugby School shows clearly how central non-school books were to school life (Fergus, 2006, appendix 3). Interestingly, Fergus' conclusions about why 'works associated with the feminine'—titles such as *Goody Two-Shoes*—should appeal to the boys, enduring such a 'harsh educational and social regime at Rugby' is that these books 'allowed boys to create an alternative home, a child's space, where they could be children in a different way than a hostile, exacting school culture permitted' (p. 241).

Moreover, in its content, the new children's literature habitually blurs the boundary between private and public education. The home was often depicted in very similar terms to school, and schools, as depicted in children's books, were very often distinctly domestic. The tone had been set by Sarah Fielding's *The Governess; or, Little Female Academy* (1749), usually accounted the first school story, in which Mrs Teachum's nine pupils are presented as a surrogate family, replacing the husband and children who have died before the opening of the book. Mrs Teachum's maternal qualities are given far more emphasis than her professional qualifications; or rather her professional qualifications *are* her maternal qualities. 'Forty Years old, tall and genteel in her Person, tho' somewhat inclined to Fat ... she had something perfectly kind and tender in her Manner' (Fielding, 1749, p. 3). This same emphasis that domesticity was essential to a good public education endured into the nineteenth century, and not only for girls' schools. Elizabeth Sandham's *The Boys' School* (1821) is even more explicit in figuring Mr Morton's school as, fundamentally, a home:

> His school was a private one for a limited number of boys; and, as he did not permit any person to assist him in the arduous task of their education, his whole time and attention were devoted to his pupils. He narrowly observed their different dispositions and tempers; and, while he slackened not his attention to their improvement in learning, he endeavoured to regulate their minds, to teach them to govern their passions, instead of allowing themselves to be governed by them; and guarded each boy from those errors to which his predominant inclination might lead him. ... Mrs Morton did her part towards making them happy: she attended to their most trifling wants with maternal solicitude. ... Having no children of their own, Mr and Mrs Morton considered their scholars as their family, and acted towards them as affectionate parents. Equal attention was paid to all; and, whatever private opinion Mr Morton might form of his pupils, he discovered no partiality, but reproved and commended each as their conduct deserved. (Sandham, 1821, p. 102)

The word 'each' carries substantial weight. The most important advantage of domestic education was that a parent or tutor would know the individual talents, and needs, of each pupil. Thus Edgeworth, holding in her hands, she says, a book used by an exemplary domestic educator, applauded the fact that 'different stories have been marked with the initials of different names by this cautious mother, who considered the temper and habits of her children, as well as their ages' (Edgeworth & Edgeworth, 1798, vol. 1, p. 322). The fear was that this individualised education would be lost at school. But Sandham's *Boys' School* promises that, if run on domestic lines, a school can still provide such personalised tuition.

Among the Abinger Papers in the Bodleian Library may be found an intriguing and entirely neglected example of the school story that further blurs the divide between public and private education. It is an incomplete manuscript apparently intended for publication by the 'Juvenile Library', the publishing firm established by Godwin and his second wife Mary Jane in 1805. It is undated and, save for a title, 'Salt Hill', written by Godwin, is in an unknown hand and its authorship remains obscure.[2] The full title reads 'Juvenile Accomplishments, or the Amusements of Salt Hill. For the Use of ~~Children~~ Schools', the deletion already betraying a certain confusion about the proper place for children's book use, or perhaps a wish for greater precision. After a 'Preface' which talks about the admirable books that have been produced 'for the perusal of children from five to ten years of age' but the lack of available material for 'boys of an age somewhat farther advanced', the text proper begins with a description of a 'little school … the like of which you see in the neighbourhood of town, with an inscription in large letters where *Young Gentlemen are boarded & taught till they are fit for Masters*', or, to be more precise, for boys 'from the age of four or five years to the age of eleven, when they were transplanted to Eton, Westminster or Harrow' (Anon, n.d., f. 1^v). One of the pupils at this school is Richard Acheson. His father 'felt an extreme anxiety for the progress of his son, & his interest in this consideration was heightened by the talents & dispositions that already discovered themselves in the mind of the boy.' It is this parental concern to fit tuition to the boy's individual aptitudes that leads him to propose a scheme for the father and son to meet periodically, along with several of his son's school friends, at the Salt Hill inn, near the school. At these meetings Mr Acheson would 'propose a question to them upon which they were to communicate their sentiments in a free & unrestrained manner' (ff. 2^r–3^r). Discussion ranges across a variety of subjects, but the manuscript gives out after a few pages.

'Salt Hill' is interesting for many reasons. It is a conduct or courtesy book for boys—and adults—that sets out the advantages of conversation flowing freely between parents and children which will 'develop their talents, their humours, their inclinations & their character' (Anon, n.d., f. 2^v–3^r). In the present context though, what is striking is its representation of Mr Acheson's good practice in refusing to relinquish the duty, and advantages, of private education even once his son has gone away to school. Here is a textual manifestation of the 'middle way' that Godwin hoped for his *Enquirer* essay, 'neither entirely public, or entirely private, avoiding the mischiefs of each, and embracing the advantages of both' (Godwin, 1797, p. 64).

3. Conclusions

There are good reasons for thinking of the children's literature of the later eighteenth and early nineteenth centuries as a product that developed to serve the demands of a growing home education market. The subjects of many of these children's books were domestic, and so was their prevailing ethos. However, what has become clear is that this new children's literature actually endorsed a more mixed economy of education. Indeed, in some instances children's books can be read as interventions in the debate on the advantages of public and private education, making the case for a pragmatic amalgam of the two. Sandham's *Boys' School*, for instance, present a model of blended public–private instruction that offers a utopian vision of the benefits of domesticated model of public schooling. Certainly, such books answered one of the chief objections to public schooling, that it could not provide the kind of personalised, needs-led education that home-schooling promised. Further, some titles represented how well a *continuum* of public and private education could function: not a supersession merely, in which children, chiefly boys, graduated from home to school as they grew older, but rather—as in *Evenings at Home* or 'Salt Hill'—an interweaving of public and private, with children able simultaneously to benefit from both parental and professional instruction. What the children's literature of this period shows us then is that the boundaries between domestic and public education were porous, and that rigid demarcation was something that was often resisted.

Disclosure statement

No potential conflict of interest was reported by the author.

Notes

1. By 1826 this tenet had become so dominant that even Edgeworth's credentials were being questioned, since she had not herself been a mother. Had she been '*Mrs* Edgeworth', 'a man of sound judgment and considerable experience' told the children's writer and educationalist Maria Budden, her books would have been worth reading. That not being the case, Budden herself 'immediately commenced her memoranda of all she tried and all she effected' in her own family, allowing her in time to produce a book that was 'the result of *twenty years*' experience in a family of six children, three sons and three daughters' (Budden, 1826, pp. v–vi).
2. It is possible Godwin was the author, employing an amanuensis, although no mention of the book is to be found in his diary or letters. It may be significant that the main text is prefaced by a letter addressed 'My dear Charles'. Godwin's step-son was Charles Clairmont, who began at Charterhouse school aged 11 in 1806. In the manuscript, Salt Hill school is for boys up to the age of 11.

References

Aikin, J., & Barbauld, A. L. (1809). *Evenings at home, or the juvenile budget opened*. 6 vols. London: J. Johnson.

Anon. (n.d.). Juvenile accomplishments, or the amusements of Salt Hill. Bodleian Library, Oxford, MS Abinger, c.25, ff. 1–12.

Anon. (1760). *A little pretty pocket-book, intended for the instruction and amusement of little Master Tommy, and pretty Miss Polly*. London: J. Newbery.

Anon. (1761). *A Present for Children*. Edinburgh: William Gray.

Anon. (1790). *Midsummer holydays, or, a long story written for the improvement and entertainment of young folk*. London: John Marshall.

Anon. (1799). *The happy family at Eason House, exhibited in the amiable conduct of the little Nelsons and their parents*. London: T. Hurst.

Anon. (1809). *Mother goose*. London: B. Tabart.

Arnold, T. (1833). *Sermons preached in the chapel of Rugby school, with an address before confirmation*. London: B. Fellowes.

Ash, J. (1760). *Grammatical institutes: or grammar, adapted to the genius of the English tongue*. London: E. and C. Dilly.

Bainbridge, J. (2015). *Storybook schools: The representation of schools and schooling in British children's fiction, 1820–1880* (Unpublished PhD thesis). University of Roehampton.

Barbauld, A. L. (1778–1779). *Lessons for children*. London: J. Johnson.

Bennett, J. (1787). *Strictures on female education; Chiefly as it relates to the culture of the heart*. London: Author.

Berquin, A. (1786). *The children's friend; Consisting of apt tales, short dialogues, and moral dramas* (Rev. Anthony Meilan, Trans). 8 vols. London: John Stockdale.

Brant, C. (2006). *Eighteenth-century letters and British culture*. Basingstoke: Palgrave Macmillan.

Broadhurst, F. (1827). A word in favour of female schools. *The Pamphleteer, 27*, 453–473.

Budden, M. (1826). *Thoughts on domestic education; the result of experience*. London: Charles Knight.

Burr, A. (1838). *The private journal of Aaron Burr, during his residence of four years in Europe* (M. L. Davis, Ed.). 2 vols. New York: Harper & Brothers.

Butler, W. (1799). *Geographical and biographical exercises, designed for the use of young ladies*. London: Author.

Campe, J. H. (1788). *The new Robinson Crusoe; an instructive and entertaining history*. 4 vols. London: John Stockdale.

Carey, J. (n.d. [1808]). *Learning better than house and land; as exemplified in the history of Harry Johnson and Dick Hobson*. London: William Darton.

Carlson, J. (2007). *England's first family of writers. Mary Wollstonecraft, William Godwin, Mary Shelley*. Baltimore: Johns Hopkins University Press.

Cohen, M. (2004). Gender and the private/public debate on education in the long eighteenth century. In R. Aldrich (Ed.), *Public or private education? Lessons from history* (pp. 15–35). London: Woburn Press.

Darwin, E. (1797). *A Plan for the conduct of female education, in boarding schools*. Derby: J. Drewry, and London: J. Johnson.

Day, T. (1783–1789). *The history of Sandford and Merton*. London: J. Stockdale.

Delaney, L. (2012). *'Making amusement the vehicle of instruction': Key developments in the nursery reading market 1783–1900* (Unpublished PhD thesis). UCL, London.

Edgeworth, M. (1796). *The parent's assistant*. London: J. Johnson.

Edgeworth, M. (2003). *The works of Maria Edgeworth. Part II* (M. Butler, Ed.). London: Pickering and Chatto.

Edgeworth, M. (2013). *Selected tales for children and young people* (S. Manly, Ed.). Basingstoke: Palgrave Macmillan.

Edgeworth, M., & Edgeworth, R. L. (1798). *Practical education.* 2 vols. London: J. Johnson.
Fanshawe, A. (1797). *Easter holidays, or domestic conversations.* Bath: S. Hazard.
Farington, J. (1924). *The Farington diary* (J. Greig, Ed.). London: Hutchinson and Co.
Fenn, E. (1783a). *Rational sports. In dialogues passing among the children of a family.* London: John Marshall.
Fenn, E. (1783b). *School occurrences: Supposed to have arisen among a set of young ladies, under the tuition of Mrs. Teachwell.* London: John Marshall.
Fergus, J. (2006). *Provincial readers in eighteenth-century England.* Oxford: Oxford University Press.
Fielding, S. (1749). *The governess; or, Little female academy.* London: Author.
Gargano, E. (2007). *Reading Victorian schoolrooms: Childhood and education in nineteenth-century fiction.* New York: Routledge.
Godwin, W. (1797). *The enquirer. Reflections on education, manners, and literature.* London: G.G. & J. Robinson.
Godwin, W. (1992). *Collected novels and memoirs of William Godwin.* Vol. 1. *Autobiography, autobiographical fragments and reflections, Godwin/Shelley correspondence, memoirs* (M. Philp, Ed.). London: William Pickering.
Grenby, M. O. (2011). *The child reader 1700–1840.* Cambridge: Cambridge University Press.
Hilton, M., & Shefrin, J. (2009). Introduction. In M. Hilton & J. Shefrin (Eds.), *Educating the child in Enlightenment Britain: Beliefs, cultures, practices* (pp. 1–20). Farnham: Ashgate.
Holt, J. (2008). *Public school literature, civic education and the politics of male adolescence.* Farnham: Ashgate.
Hughes, T. (1857). *Tom Brown's school days.* London: Macmillan.
Kilner, D. (c.1790). *Anecdotes of a boarding-school.* 2 vols. London: John Marshall.
Martineau, H. (1841). *The Crofton boys.* London: Charles Knight and Co.
Martineau, H. (1849). *Household education.* London: Edward Moxon.
May, E. (1851). *Louis' school days.* London: Binns and Goodwin.
Mill, J. S. (1981). *Collected works of John Stuart Mill.* Vol. 1. *Autobiography and literary essays* (J. M. Robson & J. Stillinger, Eds.). Toronto: University of Toronto Press.
Myers, M. (1986). Impeccable governesses, rational dames, and moral mothers: Mary Wollstonecraft and the female tradition in Georgian children's books. *Children's Literature, 14,* 31–59.
Navest, K. M. (2011). *John Ash and the rise of the children's grammar* (Unpublished PhD thesis). Universiteit Leiden, Leiden.
Pullen, H. W. (1874). *The ground ash: a public school story.* London: Simpkin, Marshall.
Richardson, A. (2002). Mary Wollstonecraft on education. In C. L. Johnson (Ed.), *The Cambridge companion to Mary Wollstonecraft* (pp. 24–41). Cambridge: Cambridge University Press.
Salzmann, C. G. (1790). *Elements of morality, for the use of children* (M. Wollstonecraft, Trans.). 2 vols. London: J. Johnson.
Sandham, E. (1821). *The boys' school; or Traits of character in early life.* London: John Souter.
Semple, E. (1804). *Gertrude, Agnes and Melite, and Amelia Douglas.* London: J. Harris.
Sewell, E. M. (1846–1848). *Laneton Parsonage. A tale for children on the practical use of a portion of the Church catechism.* London: Longman, Brown, Green, and Longmans.
Skedd, S. (1997). Women teachers and the expansion of girls' schooling in England c.1760–1820. In H. Barker & E. Chalus (Eds.), *Gender in eighteenth-century England: Roles, representation and responsibilities* (pp. 101–125). London: Longman.
Smith, E. L. (2008). Centering the home-garden: The arbor, wall, and gate in moral tales for children. *Children's Literature, 36,* 24–48.
Trimmer, S. (1780). *An easy introduction to the knowledge of nature, and reading the holy scriptures.* London: Author.

Trimmer, S. (1782–1785). *Sacred history selected from the scriptures.* 6 vols. London: J. Dodsley et al.

Trimmer, S. (1786). *Fabulous histories. Designed for the instruction of children, respecting their treatment of animals.* London: T. Longman et al.

Vaux, F. B. (1816). *Domestic pleasures; or, the happy fire-side.* London: Darton, Harvey and Darton.

Walker, G. (1813). *The adventures of Timothy Thoughtless: or, the misfortunes of a little boy who ran away from boarding-school.* London: G. Walker.

Watkins, L. (1813). *The history and adventures of little James and Mary.* London: Dean & Munday.

Whyman, S. (2009). *The pen and the people. English letter writers 1660–1800.* Oxford: Oxford University Press.

Wollstonecraft, M. (1792). *A vindication of the rights of woman: With strictures on political and moral subjects.* London: J. Johnson.

Woodley, S. (2009). 'Oh miserable and most ruinous measure': The debate between private and public education in Britain 1760–1800. In M. Hilton & J. Shefrin (Eds.), *Educating the child in Enlightenment Britain: Beliefs, cultures, practices* (pp. 21–39). Farnham: Ashgate.

Wynne, J. H. (1784). *Choice emblems, natural, historical, fabulous, moral, and divine ... For the use of schools.* Cotsen Children's Library, Princeton University, Eng 18/Newbery 152958.

Education in the working-class home: modes of learning as revealed by nineteenth-century criminal records

Rosalind Crone
The Open University, UK

The transmission of knowledge and skills within the working-class household greatly troubled social commentators and social policy experts during the first half of the nineteenth century. To prove theories which related criminality to failures in working-class up-bringing, experts and officials embarked upon an ambitious collection of data on incarcerated criminals at various penal institutions. One such institution was the County Gaol at Ipswich. The exceptionally detailed information that survives on families, literacy, education and apprenticeships of the men, women and children imprisoned there has the potential to transform our understanding of the nature of home schooling (broadly interpreted) amongst the working classes in nineteenth-century England. This article uses data sets from prison registers to chart both the incidence and 'success' of instruction in reading and writing within the domestic environment. In the process, it highlights the importance of schooling in working-class families, but also the potentially growing significance of the family in occupational training.

The family has proved to be an elusive agent in the transmission of knowledge and skills amongst the working classes in nineteenth-century England. Contemporaries were convinced of its importance. Until at least the 1860s, the moral condition of the working-class family was held responsible for a range of social ills, from popular insurrection to rising crime rates (Godfrey & Lawrence, 2005; Wiener, 1990). But despite attention devoted to the subject by the new statistical societies and a growing number of social policy 'experts', the extent and nature of education (broadly defined) within the home remained largely hidden from view. Social historians have been similarly aware of the presence of the family and the need to explain its role in instructing its members in useful and essential skills. Large quantitative sources, such as census enumerators' books, parish registers (births, marriages, deaths), settlement examinations and apprenticeship indentures, reveal much about family structure, but tell us little about relationships, communication, forms of nurturing and teaching. These gaps and silences have led historians at different times to be both emphatic about and dismissive of the educative role played by the family (Anderson, 1972; Lane, 1996; Levine, 1979; Mitch, 1992; Snell, 1985; Vincent, 1989).

Using qualitative or descriptive sources, namely accounts by working-class men (and a handful of women) of their lives, either written on their own impetus or given in response to investigations conducted by journalists, social investigators and officials, historians have been able to present a convincing outline of the 'domestic curriculum' in the working-class household. Some of what was learnt by family members was incidental, largely the result of absorption, observation or imitation, for example, learning to crawl or speak, developing an awareness and later knowledge of identity and community, and cultivating and expanding the imaginative faculties. Of those skills and forms of knowledge that required direct tuition, we have been told that moral values were imparted and literary skills increasingly taught, but that sons were sent away from the home to learn a trade (Humphries, 2010; Vincent, 1989). There are, however, significant problems in the use of such sources. The representativeness of the authors, as typically male and from a particular social group (autodidacts) is questionable, and the narrative conventions employed cast some doubt on their accuracy.

My research, based on a quantitative source—the Registers from Ipswich County Gaol in Suffolk—provides new insight on the content of the domestic curriculum. Between 1840 and 1870, every man, woman and child brought to Ipswich Gaol, having been convicted of or awaiting trial for a crime committed in the administrative district of East Suffolk, had personal information recorded in the Register. Over the course of the 30 years, the Registers were filled with 14,026 records about 10,441 offenders and 14,368 separate charges (or 12,885 unique offences). Just about every prison in England during this period had registers to capture information about inmates, but the registers designed for the two County Gaols in Suffolk (Ipswich and Bury St Edmunds) seem to have been fairly unique in terms of the quantity of information recorded about each incarcerated individual. Moreover, at Ipswich Gaol the officials demonstrated a substantial level of commitment to the collection of information and the amount of detail they included was exceptional. Thus, for every prisoner, we are told their name, residence, occupation (and if a trade where they learnt it), age, height, complexion, health, distinguishing marks, place of birth, father's name and residence, marital status, spouse's residence and means of subsistence, number of offspring and their ages; we are given information on their offence, trial, punishment and previous crimes; and we are told whether they had served in the armed forces, could read and write, and had gone to school and for how long. Alongside this information about individuals, the Registers tell us about families, namely 255, where multiple members had committed offences, mostly together but also separately.

The potential offered by these Registers appears enormous, but caution must be exercised in the use of such data to expose patterns in the experience of the general population. Offenders who came into contact with the nineteenth-century criminal justice system were overwhelmingly male (in the case of Ipswich Gaol, 86% of offenders were men), and typically aged between 16 and 30 (63%; or in comparison with the 1851 census, 71% of prisoners were aged between 16 and 30 compared with 25% of the county's population). They were also most likely to come from the poorest levels of society; 59% of offenders at Ipswich were unskilled workers (or the daughters of unskilled workers), overwhelmingly described as 'labourers'. To put this in context: the 1851 census found that 28% of the population in Suffolk worked as labourers (agricultural and general), or 40% of those aged between 15 and 30; in comparison, 62% of the male prisoner cohort for 1851 worked in unskilled occupations, or 70% of those males aged between 15 and 30. Most of the offenders in the Ipswich Registers cannot be described as members of a 'hardened criminal class'. The great majority were arrested for: petty thefts (35%), a crime which could often be described as a strategy to supplement meagre incomes or cope with periods of unemployment (Davis, 1989; Gatrell, 1989); poaching (10%), a possible exertion of customary rights but at the very least action largely condoned by the local community (Glyde, 1856; Hay, 1975; Osborne & Winstanley, 2006); low level assaults (9%), a traditional method of dispute resolution (Wood, 2004); public order or moral offences (4%, and not including damage to property), many of which were new crimes under laws enforced by new police forces; and crimes associated with poverty (18%), such as vagrancy, misbehaviour in the workhouse, and failure to maintain one's family. Despite the 'ordinariness' of their criminal behaviour, it remains a challenging task to isolate those characteristics associated with their criminality and those common to Suffolk's labouring poor.

Moreover, like most nineteenth-century sources which appear to lend themselves to quantification, the data are far from perfect. The design of forms and compilation of statistics were in their infancy in the mid-nineteenth century, and terms used in categories were often variable (Cullen, 1975; Dobraszczyk, 2009). Therefore a degree of data wrangling is required to extract usable statistics from the Registers. To further complicate matters, 18% of offenders appeared more than once (but usually no more than twice) in the Registers, and there is a degree of fluidity in the profiles of a substantial number, either because their lives had changed (they had married, moved parish, changed occupation or acquired or lost literate skills) or because errors were made, by the clerk or prisoner, deliberate or accidental, in the collection of information.

In spite of all these caveats, this article will use the unique collection of data on the family, literacy, schooling and occupation contained in the Ipswich Registers to expose several important aspects of the domestic curriculum while testing existing theories about the role played by the family in instructing its members. It sheds new light on the role of domestic instruction in the transmission of literacy, of occupational skills and of criminal expertise at least in the rural county of Suffolk, and potentially in England more generally, during the nineteenth century.

I. Literate skills

Alongside improvements in public health, religiously-sponsored elementary education was regarded by social policy experts as a panacea for a range of social ills, including rising crime rates. As Vincent has written, 'those who campaigned for intervention, by church and then state … based their appeal on a denunciation of training provided in the homes of the labouring poor' (Vincent, 1989, p. 73). Contemporary campaigners collected statistics on the educational attainments of criminals in order to justify and increase government expenditure on elementary education. However, these proved more difficult to interpret than expected. When examined against marriage register evidence, as well as local studies of literacy within working-class communities, the prisoners' skills broadly matched those of the communities from which they came (Crone, 2010; Nicholas, 1990; and see BRO Q/SO20; Mayhew et al., 1862).

Literacy rates generally in the primarily rural county of Suffolk lagged behind national figures for most of the nineteenth century. With regard to the prisoners at Ipswich Gaol, although the literacy rate of the men was well below that of the county for the period 1840–1870 (determined by the marriage registers), this difference was expected given the over representation of the labouring poor in the sample, the prisoners' literacy matched the steady increase of that of Suffolk's males over the course of the 30 years (Suffolk from 52% to 69%; prisoners from 25.7% to 53.7%, or prisoners of average marital age from 24.5% to 53.4%), and the prisoners' literacy always exceeded the benchmarks for unskilled occupations provided by scholars such as Vincent (1844–1849, 42.2% compared with 31%, 1854–1859, 44.9% compared with 41%, 1864–1869, 55.7% compared with 51%). The small numbers of women in each yearly cohort of prisoners, especially those of marital age, generate variable results, but the average rates of literacy for women aged between 21 and 30 across five year periods also compare favourably with those of the daughters of unskilled workers analysed by Vincent (1844–1849, 23.8% for the prisoners compared with 33%, 1854–1859, 47.9% compared with 48%, and 1864–1869, 62.1% compared with 61%) (Vincent, 1989, pp. 97 and 102). Moreover the average rate of literacy amongst the female prisoners overtook that of the male prisoners at roughly the same time as in the county population (late 1850s).

Awareness of the similarities between prisoners' literacy rates and those of local labouring populations led members of the nineteenth-century statistical societies to establish a new dividing line between those who could neither read nor write, who could only read, or who could read and write *imperfectly*, and those who could read and write well, or who had a superior education, the rationale being that the former group had not attended school, or had not attended *for long enough* to have received a proper, moral education. The new dividing line produced the desired result, as few prisoners (and probably few working-class men and women) could be said to have received a superior education (Fletcher, 1843, 1847, 1849; Porter, 1837; Rawson, 1841).

The intense focus on the level of skills achieved as an indicator of schooling led a number of enthusiastic individuals—gaol chaplains, surgeon superintendents on convict ships, and officials in charge of specific prisons—to compile their own sets of data on the schooling history of those under their care (see, for example, TNA, ADM101/13/9, ff.2–5, ADM101/16/2, ff. 12, MT32/2; BRO Q/SO 24 & 25, 1854–1857). Matched up with information on the skills acquired, these data sets have the potential to reveal a great deal about the schooling of the labouring poor in the 100 years preceding the 1870 Education Act. The County Gaol at Ipswich was one institution where such data were collected. Incarcerated men, women and children were questioned not only about their elementary skills, but also about where they had been to school and for how long. A wide variety of information was entered into this category by the gaol clerks. Not only do the Registers tell us about the men, women and children who had learnt to read or read and write at church-sponsored day schools, free schools, grammar schools, dame schools, Sunday schools and so on (52% of males and 63% of females), but they also draw attention to those who had learnt their skills as adults, for example, in military schools and prison schools, and, most importantly, reveal those who exclusively learnt their skills in informal settings (predominantly the home) or who 'taught themselves'.

Historians have placed a great deal of emphasis on the role of the family in imparting literate skills. Vincent has argued that literacy was an increasingly 'common element in the overall [domestic] curriculum as the nineteenth century progressed', though also acknowledges that 'it always had to compete with a wide range of skills which had equal or greater priority' (Vincent, 1989, p. 56). Vincent and Raey have used nineteenth-century surveys to highlight the substantial presence of books in working-class homes, not only religious texts but also primers and spelling books (Raey, 1991; Vincent, 1983, 1989). Most recently, Humphries, on the basis of evidence in working-class autobiographies, declared that a crucial strategy for education was home teaching, and foremost among the domestic instructors were mothers, who were both 'more available' and more ambitious for their children. Brothers, sisters and grandparents 'also taught basic literacy, strengthening sibling and inter-generational ties'. But notably absent in many cases were fathers, which led Humphries to conclude that although 'some fathers taught their children … many were too busy earning their family's living to provide instruction, and in the throes of the industrial revolution less time became available' (Humphries, 2010, p. 320).

Admittedly, the presence of the family continues to loom large in the records of those prisoners where there is no direct reference to it. Some 261 prisoners with at least one literate skill failed to provide any information about how they had acquired their ability, and a further 30 specifically stated in response to the question of where they had been schooled, 'not any where'. Given the level of detail on the overwhelming majority, it is difficult to make assumptions about the role played by the family in these cases. Furthermore, attending school was not a bar to domestic instruction. One female offender, arrested in 1840 for an unknown crime but not convicted, claimed that although she had been at church school for a short time, her father had taught her to read (Suffolk Record Office, A609/1(31) ff.57). Fifteen offenders on different appearances at the gaol claimed to have been to school and to have taught themselves the literate skills. In some cases it is clear that they learnt to read at school and later taught themselves to write. Others might have re-taught themselves skills they had previously learnt at school but lost through a lack of practice. A significant number of prisoners who attended school (just under 40%) claimed they went for periods of two years or less, and it is conceivable that many of these had some familial support. Similarly, those who described long periods of schooling may have only attended intermittently and had parents who helped fill the gaps. The poor quality of instruction delivered at many schools was emphasised by autodidact autobiographies and social commentators (Glyde, 1856; Griffin, 2013).

However, explicit evidence on the family contained in the Registers calls into question the role it played in imparting the literate skills. First, data on the presence of the skills within the 255 family groups identified confirmed the haphazardness or randomness with which literate skills were passed from parents to children, a state of affairs which Levine also identified in his study of Shepshed, Leicestershire, at the turn of the nineteenth century. Not all literate artisans, tradesmen and labourers could arrange for all their children to acquire these skills (Levine, 1979; Vincent, 1989). All sorts of combinations of literacy were present amongst groups of family members at Ipswich Gaol. In the case of the Dranes, convicted for poaching in 1867, father James could read and write but his son had neither skill (Suffolk Record Office, A609/26 ff.396, 397). Similarly, with regard to members of the Williams family, arrested for stealing items from a dwelling house in 1853, father John could read and write but both his daughters, Mary Ann and Ellen, were wholly illiterate (Suffolk Record Office, A609/14 ff.366, 367, 368). And brothers John and Robert Steggall, convicted for poaching in 1841, also had different literacy profiles, the former wholly illiterate, the latter able to read and write (Suffolk Record Office, A609/1(31) ff.316, 317). Parallel examples are littered throughout the Registers across the whole period.

Parents made decisions about whether their children would acquire the literate skills. The Ipswich Gaol Registers tell us that when they decided in the affirmative, they invariably made use of local schools. Of the 68% of offenders who possessed at least one of the literate skills (for our purposes, we shall refer to both the partially literate and fully literate as 'literate'), more than 90% had attended school for a period of time. A handful of illiterate prisoners also claimed to have attended school, a reminder of the potential fragility of the literate skills.

The flip side of this is that very few prisoners claimed to have acquired their literate skills through informal forms of education *exclusively*. The level of detail contained in the Registers allows us to be quite specific about their experiences. Fifteen prisoners claimed to have been instructed in the literate skills while 'in service', either during an apprenticeship, or as a servant, or as a 'bound' labourer. Although informal, because this type of instruction was linked with work, these prisoners cannot be included in an analysis of 'domestic education'. Barely 1% of 'literate' offenders, or a total of 90 men and women, were entirely 'home schooled', meaning that these prisoners explicitly stated that they had been taught to read, or to read and write, by family members (66) or friends (23), so not just within a domestic environment but also by instructors with whom they had intimate relationships. Some 167 offenders, roughly 2.5% of those who were 'literate', claimed to have taught themselves the literate skills. These men and women would likely have acquired their skills during time away from work, probably within a domestic environment, and most likely with the help of family and friends. Moreover, during the 1860s, it is likely that those who were 'home schooled' were described as 'self taught' by the gaol officials, as direct references to home schooling disappeared from the Registers in this period. At least one repeat offender who claimed to have been home schooled when arrested in 1850 was subsequently described as 'self taught' on his return to the gaol in 1859 (Suffolk Record Office, A609/9 ff.395). It seems sensible then, while acknowledging key differences between the home schooled and self taught, to consider these two categories together in the analysis.

While it is true that the small numbers in both risk the sample being statistically insignificant, it is still possible to draw some conclusions from the offenders' experiences. Proportionately, more 'literate' females were home schooled than 'literate' males, but the margin separating the genders was slight: for example, in the case of 'literate' males, around 1% were home schooled and just over 2% were self taught, while in the case of 'literate' females, just over 1% were home schooled and around 3% were self taught. Occupation did not seem to be related to home schooling either. Those in unskilled occupations (or with unskilled fathers) were slightly over represented among the home schooled (67% compared with 59% in the Registers as a whole). In contrast, the occupational breakdown of those 'self taught' roughly matched that of all offenders (self taught skilled being 22% compared with 25%, and unskilled self taught 52% compared with 59%). There was no correlation between home schooling and domestic instruction in occupational skills; 81% of those who were taught a trade at home were sent out to school to learn their literate skills, an almost identical proportion to those who served an apprenticeship outside the home (83%). Similarly, just under 2% of those who learnt their trade at home also learnt their literate skills at home, and only 1% of those who were sent away for their apprenticeship learnt their literate skills at home.

Figure 1 shows the proportion of offenders home schooled, 'self taught' and sent to school in each birth cohort (where available). At first glance, these figures highlight the decline of home schooling from the 1830s onwards, matching a growth in the proportion sent to school (which reached a plateau of around 60%). Other sources also suggest that the foundation of elementary schools increased in Suffolk from the 1830s onwards (*Digest of Parochial Returns*, 1819; *Education Enquiry*, 1835; Glyde, 1856). However, these statistics need some contextualisation to be analysed correctly. Small numbers in several birth cohorts—1760s (10),

HOME EDUCATION IN HISTORICAL PERSPECTIVE

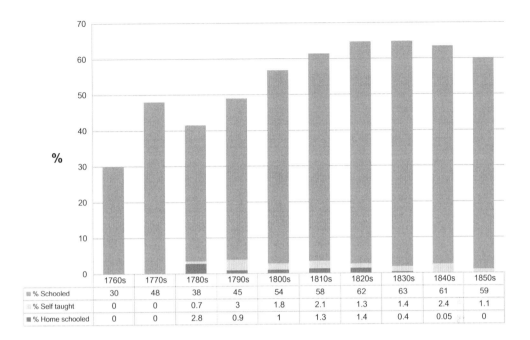

Figure 1. Type of education matched with birth cohorts of offenders

1770s (29) and 1780s (140)—skew the data and should be disregarded. The proportion of those 'self taught' needs to be taken into consideration. Those imprisoned during the 1860s were most likely to have been born in the 1830s, 1840s and 1850s; the growing proportion of those self taught in these three decades alongside the decline in the number 'home schooled' confirms that a significant number who were home schooled in these decades were described by officials as self taught. Thus, if we add together the proportion home schooled and self taught across the period 1790–1859, the percentage of offenders who learnt their skills outside the classroom (and probably at home) was remarkably consistent, hovering between 2 and 3%. The growth of schools and expansion of literacy made little difference to this steady group.

Location information provided by offenders—place of residence, birth, father's residence and schooling—can be used somewhat to help us understand the decisions made by parents in the schooling of their offspring. It is by no means perfect. The offenders, on the whole, were a mobile group. Of those born in Suffolk, 48% were resident in a different parish from that in which they were born. However, more than 60% of schooled offenders were sent to a school in their birth parish; 63% of offenders aged 15 and under were still resident in their birth parish; and the profiles of repeat offenders who were married with children aged 10 and under did show a greater tendency to stay resident in the same parish (63% did not move parishes between appearances). Therefore it seems reasonable to try to understand what factors might have encouraged home schooling by looking at the state of education within offenders' birth parishes.

HOME EDUCATION IN HISTORICAL PERSPECTIVE

Two nineteenth-century education censuses—in 1818 and 1833—provided lists of schools that existed in each parish of Suffolk (*Digest of Parochial Returns*, 1819; *Education Enquiry*, 1835). Information on schools in parishes in which home schooled offenders were born (more specifically, those who would have been home schooled in childhood) was extracted from each census. That from the 1818 census was examined alongside the schooling data of all offenders born in the relevant parishes between 1780 and 1818, and that for the 1833 census was similarly examined alongside those offenders born between 1820 and 1839. Both cohorts contained examples where home schooled offenders came from small parishes which had no schools. Similarly, the schooling profiles of all offenders compared with the 1833 census suggested that the capacity of the existing parish schools could also be an important factor (Iken had just one Sunday school, and only one of 15 offenders were schooled in the parish, compared with Weybread, which had four day schools and one Sunday school, and 6 of 10 offenders were schooled in the parish). Although it could be argued that these circumstances created a need for exclusive home schooling, the presence of offenders from the same birth cohorts who were sent to schools in neighbouring parishes prevents us from making any generalisations. Religion could have played a part in parents' decision to home school their children. The home-schooled offenders from Barham and Mendlesham, parishes which had Church of England Sunday schools, were Dissenters. Again, we cannot generalise from the experiences of this man and woman, though a larger study on the schooling of offenders who were Dissenters might prove or disprove a pattern of active avoidance of establishment schools. In sum, the even split between the presence of the home schooled in parishes with high levels of illiteracy and no schools and parishes with high levels of literacy and multiple schools, suggests that individual circumstances and choices, rather than overarching social conditions, seem to have been the primary determinant for home schooling.

Finally, the Registers provide evidence on the quality of instruction received at home and the likely identity of the instructor. The majority of the home schooled only learnt to read and not to write (72% and 28%, respectively). Compared with all 'literate' offenders (of whom 34% could only read and 66% could read and write), readers were over represented amongst the home schooled. With regard to those self taught, the reading skill was still dominant (52%), but not to such a great extent, particularly among males (48% could only read). While it is true that the achievements of the pupil were limited by the skills of the instructor (Vincent, 1989), it is impossible to demonstrate with the available data (prison and marriage registers, not to mention autobiographies) that the partial literacy of parents was a correlative for home schooling amongst the working classes. It is conceivable that those parents who had found that the reading skill was both useful and adequate might have been content to pass on that skill to their children but have seen no reason to send their children to school to learn to write, especially where resources were tight. Or that restrictions on time within the domestic environment necessarily restricted instruction to the skill of reading. These are suppositions. Yet we can argue that the overwhelming proportion of readers amongst the home schooled again emphasises the marginality of exclusive home schooling during the nineteenth century. From mid-century, an increasing number of institutions were instructing pupils in both skills. This matches data from gaols across the country which show that the partially literate were a rapidly shrinking group from the 1850s onwards (Crone, 2010). If exclusive home schooling was more widespread or common, we might have expected the partial literates to show a greater resilience.

According to the evidence in the gaol Registers, the transmission of the literate skills occurred primarily within the nuclear family (of the 90 home schooled, only three identified instructors from the extended family, an aunt, an uncle and a grandmother). Also, the direction of that transmission was predominantly downwards, as skills were passed from one generation to the next (only two prisoners claimed to have learnt to read from their children, and four offenders to read, or to read and write, from their siblings). Six husbands learnt to read (three) or to read and write (three) from their wives, but no husbands taught their wives the literate skills. This matches the gender inversion with regard to literacy that existed in rural counties such as Suffolk (Vincent, 1989). Most importantly, 47 of the 90 offenders claimed their parents had been their instructors, and 30 identified a specific parent. Their evidence suggests that fathers did teach their sons (17 of 20); and only three daughters were exclusively taught by their fathers. Mothers also taught their sons (8 of 10); and there were only two examples of daughters exclusively taught by their mothers. In fact, if we look at the 19 women who were home schooled, all bar one were taught the literate skills by their parents, and most often both parents played a role. This is in contrast to the male offenders in the group, whose profiles overall were more diverse, but where men were taught by their parents it was more likely that one parent took responsibility for their instruction. This evidence links rather neatly to that on formal schooling. Although proportionately more female offenders had attended school than male offenders (63% compared with 52%), males who attended school were substantially more likely to learn both literate skills than their female counterparts (69% compared with 52%). In other words, where resources were allocated to the education of males, either within or outside the home, the outcomes were more substantial.

II. Occupational skills

Occupation by itself was not regarded as a cause of crime by contemporaries; rather, a refusal to work, as well as a preference for profligate lifestyles which encouraged the misuse of any honest earnings, were defined as the principal characteristics of criminality (Godfrey & Lawrence, 2005). Parents were held responsible for failing to instil a good work ethic. Commentators and experts thus had little to say about the acquisition of occupational skills within the home, though many believed that instruction in a trade was an essential rehabilitative mechanism, especially for juvenile offenders.

Historians have been similarly vague about the nature of occupational instruction within the working-class home in part because of a lack of evidence, but also because most unskilled jobs did not require labourers to have an existing skill set: children were sent out to work from an early age, and often what they needed to know was learnt on the job. With regard to skilled occupations which did require specific training typically through apprenticeships, historians have afforded a role to parents in selecting a trade for their sons and sometimes even a master under whom to serve, but have stressed that it was relatively rare for sons to complete their apprenticeships at home. Parish settlement laws dictated that artisans and tradesmen could only acquire legal settlement by their own right through apprenticeship outside their father's parish of settlement. Hence apprenticeship to one's own father led to a failure to settle in their own right (Snell, 1985). Moreover, rather than passing on the family business, fathers often found it more useful to place sons in complementary trades, or, in the case of traditional handicrafts where sons sometimes did succeed their fathers, there remained a tendency to send boys away for their apprenticeships in order that they might learn the latest techniques. Humphries concluded that such practices were a testament to 'English apprenticeship's resilience to entropy. It was an outward-looking institution which allowed boys to advance themselves and not just fill their fathers' boots' (Humphries, 2010, p. 273). Apprenticeship indentures suggest that some parents looked to place their sons with extended family members as this could be both easier and cheaper (Lane, 1996). However, through close examination of working-class narratives, Humphries found that the vast majority, around 76% of apprentices, served under masters outside the family (compared with 9% under their own fathers), and that those boys apprenticed to either distant kin or non-relatives went on to achieve greater success (Humphries, 2010).

The Ipswich Gaol Registers provide new insights on occupational training within the home. Offenders who arrived at Ipswich Gaol were not only asked how they earned a living, but, in the case of artisans and tradesmen, they were also asked where they learnt their trade and from whom. Not all provided details of their apprenticeships; 44% of those in skilled and 13% of those in semi-skilled occupations gave this information to the clerks. This is not necessarily an indication of how many tradesmen served apprenticeships, even though this was a period in which apprenticeships were in decline and many semi-skilled trades did not require apprenticeships to be served. Only three offenders across the 30 year period specifically stated that they had not served apprenticeships. Moreover, there is little evidence to suggest that the family, as a provider of occupational training, is hiding in the gaps and silences. Of those skilled and semi-skilled offenders who did not provide any apprenticeship information, only 8.5% and 14% respectively shared the same occupation as their fathers.

In practice, 1284 offenders (including six females) served 1289 apprenticeships. The disparity between these figures arises from the fact that six offenders claimed they had served multiple apprenticeships, two in the same trade, one in a related trade and three in different trades. Some 212 offenders (16%) specifically stated that they learnt their trade at home, primarily from their father (only eight learnt from brothers and one from a grandfather), while 525 (41%), who gave the names of masters together with places where they served their apprenticeships, had obviously been sent away. Some 552 (43%) only gave the name of the parish in which they learnt their trades. However, using surrounding information about these offenders, we can make some adjustments to the figures. Of those who were sent away, 19 shared the same surname as their masters, so it is likely that these men were sent to extended family members (following Lane's interpretation of apprenticeship indentures (Lane, 1996, p. 10)). Of those who gave only the name of the parish where they served their apprenticeship, 72 were not only in the same occupation as their fathers, but also served their apprenticeship in either their parish of birth or their father's parish of residence. That these men learnt their trade from their fathers is a reasonable assumption; the profiles of repeat offenders confirm this—while on one visit to the gaol these men stated that they had been apprenticed to their fathers, on other visits (either earlier or later) only the name of the parish in which they served was given. Some 193 went into a trade which was different from their father's. With this evidence the Gaol Books tell us that 54% of skilled tradesmen (100% of tradeswomen) were apprenticed out, 22% were apprenticed to their fathers and 2% were sent to relatives (leaving the circumstances of 22% unknown).

This 22% (even 16%) is not an insignificant proportion. Furthermore, it could still be an underestimate. One of the six offenders who claimed to have served multiple apprenticeships was Frederick Read, a shoemaker who hailed from Framlingham. On his first conviction in 1846 aged 22, Read stated that he had learnt his trade from his father, but on his second conviction in 1848 he said that he had been apprenticed to King at Framlingham (Suffolk Record Office, A609/5 ff.414, A609/7 ff.268). This contradiction could be the result of prisoner error, but there was neither an obvious motivation nor more general evidence to suggest that some prisoners provided false information. So Read might very well have started his apprenticeship at home and finished it under a non-relative. Unfortunately, the Registers cannot tell us how common that practice might have been.

The proportion of offenders who served apprenticeships within their immediate families far exceeds that of other studies, namely Humphries (2010) (9%). It could be argued that those who learnt their trade at home were over represented in the prison population, further proof of Humphries' conclusion that those apprenticed to strangers fared better in life. If this were the case, we might expect to see an increase in the number apprenticed to their fathers among the 239 repeat offenders who gave details of their apprenticeships, but there was none (24%). In the absence of other quantitative studies on apprenticeships within the home it remains difficult to prove either way.

Proceeding on the basis that the prisoners' experience of apprenticeship was broadly representative of that of tradesmen generally, the data in the Registers reveal some important patterns. Table 1 shows the proportion of men apprenticed within and outside the home for each birth cohort captured by the Registers. The

HOME EDUCATION IN HISTORICAL PERSPECTIVE

Table 1. Apprenticeship patterns in each birth cohort of offenders

Birth cohort	Total number	% apprenticed to non kin	% apprenticed within the nuclear family	% apprenticed to extended family
1760s	3	66	33	0
1770s	5	40	40	0
1780s	17	71	6	6
1790s	45	40	22	4
1800s	108	60	17	2
1810s	221	58	18	1
1820s	416	55[b]	26	2
1830s	288[a]	52[c]	29	1
1840s	163	49[d]	21	0
1850s	17	59	18	0

Notes: The table excludes offenders (five in total) whose birth cohorts were unknown. For the six offenders who served multiple apprenticeships, details of all their apprenticeships are included in the data.
[a]One offender taught his trade in prison not included in this decade.
[b]Included are two offenders who learnt trades at the workhouse.
[c]Included are seven offenders who learnt trades at the workhouse.
[d]Includes one offender who learnt his trade at the reformatory.

decades 1760s–1790s and the 1850s contain too few offenders to provide robust statistics. However, a pattern is evident between the years 1800 and 1849, whereby the proportion of those instructed within the nuclear family increased matching a decrease in the proportion sent away for apprenticeships. The decrease is expected. Although historians disagree on the cause and precise dates, and significant regional variation existed, it is clear that apprenticeship had fallen into decline by the early nineteenth century (Lane, 1996; Snell, 1985). However, historians have been largely silent on alternative means by which tradesmen acquired their skills; for example, few, if any, have suggested that the home became a more important training centre.

The 1284 offenders came from a diverse range of occupations, 155 different trades to be precise. Many trades were very specialised or unusual and so were represented by just one or two offenders, for example, screw cutters, scale beam makers, pipe makers, anchor smiths, and so on. With regard to those trades which were represented by 10 or more offenders, even where the proportion of men who were sent to members of the extended family was taken into account, there was not one trade where the proportion of offenders who were taught within the family exceeded the proportion sent to non-kin.

Finally, Figure 2 plots the proportion of offenders apprenticed out and instructed at home from the six most prominent trades across the period 1800–1849 (the dates representing the prisoners' birth cohorts). The small numbers which result from scattering the offenders in this way created some very noisy data. At least one trade, shoemaking, showed no clear pattern whatsoever. Still, there were some significant trends of which we should take note. In the case of both blacksmiths and tailors, the proportion sent away to serve an apprenticeship

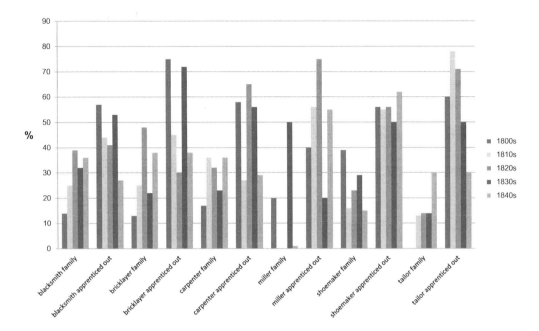

Figure 2. Apprenticeship patterns in six trades across five birth cohorts

declined over the period, while the proportion kept at home demonstrated a matching increase. The data for the carpenters were more difficult to interpret, but we could argue that the nuclear family became more important in providing apprenticeships to its members if the 1830s represents an anomaly. The 1830s also appear to have been an anomaly for millers and bricklayers. With regard to the former, disregarding the 1830s revealed a pattern of sending sons out for apprenticeships. As for the bricklayers, the general downward curve in indentured apprenticeships, which was not matched by a rise of the family as provider, could be indicative of the worsening state of the trade. Bricklayers were victims of industrialisation and deskilling, as many agricultural labourers took to bricklaying when work was available, and hence we might expect some instability in the data concerning those who continued to learn the trade (Snell, 1985).

Because the data on the 1284 offenders tells us about the experiences of those who served apprenticeships, and not about those tradesmen or artisans who did not, the Ipswich Gaol Books cannot tell us about the speed of the overall decline of apprenticeship in nineteenth-century Suffolk. But if we take the decline for granted, the Gaol Books do tell us something about the shape and character of this decline. Crucially, they suggest that the role of the nuclear family, in providing instruction in trades, gradually increased as the number of men sent away to serve apprentices slowly declined. This, together with the significant overall proportion of those who served apprenticeships (predominantly) under their fathers (more than one-fifth), strongly indicates that more attention needs to be given to the transmission of occupational skills within the nineteenth-century working-class home.

III. Criminal skills

As noted above, the evidence drawn on in this study was produced in response to contemporary fears about the moral condition of the working-class family, or, more specifically, the lack of moral instruction delivered by parents to their children which encouraged the latter to indulge in idleness, enjoy profligate lifestyles, and commit crime. Some commentators even went so far as to argue that criminal parents produced criminal children, not only through the bad examples they set, but also by schooling their offspring in criminal techniques (Glyde, 1856; *Select Committee*, 1828, p. 48; Wiener, 1990). Research by social historians has shown that, on the contrary, moral instruction was a key part of the 'domestic curriculum' (Raey, 1991; Vincent, 1983, 1989). The homes of criminals were not an exception to the rule. In their accounts of their offending behaviour, adult prisoners rarely held their parents responsible, and more often than not emphasised the efforts of parents to provide moral (typically religious) instruction and guidance (Browning, 1847; Joseph, 1853; Kingsmill, 1854). The statements made by juvenile offenders to penal officials during the 1830s similarly suggest that delinquency was rarely a product of specific parenting styles or corruption. Instead, where a correlation between family life and crime seemed evident, offending behaviour was caused by parental neglect which resulted from external stresses on family life, such as poverty, unemployment, death, disease and poor housing (Shore, 1999). The sole historical study on intergenerational offending patterns, which traced the ancestors and descendants of 68 persistent offenders (>five convictions) who appeared before the Petty Sessions Court at Crewe, Cheshire, between 1880 and 1940, also found that criminal parents did not necessarily produce criminal children. The transmission of offending behaviour between generations was more likely incidental, the product of the effects of social upheaval (Godfrey, Cox, & Farrall, 2007).

Evidence from the Ipswich Gaol Registers supports these conclusions while adding yet another specific dimension—that the working-class family was not a site for criminal instruction. This was demonstrated primarily through the analysis of information on accomplices in the Registers. Between 1840 and 1870, just over 8% of crimes in the Ipswich Gaol Books had multiple suspects attached to them (1153). Of that 8%, only 18% (198) were committed by groups of family members, or groups containing family members. In terms of familial relationships within those groups, the overwhelming presence of the nuclear family is, again, impossible to ignore. Although familial relationships between offenders were retrospectively identified, and therefore reliant on the details of *immediate* family provided in individual records (name and occupation of father, ages of children, circumstance of the spouse, and so on), allowing for this did not change the outcome. For example, only 34 additional groups contained members with the same surname. In 20 of these, the individuals most likely had an immediate familial relationship; the level of detail provided was not specific enough to confirm the relationship beyond doubt. Of the remaining 14, in only one case did the familial information supplied strongly suggest an extended familial relationship: in 1843, Elizabeth Bailey was arrested with her (probably) daughter in law, for stealing pork from a dwelling house at Rickinghall. Neither was convicted for the crime (Suffolk Record Office, A609/2 ff.97, 98). Still, if we defined all 14 as extended family groups, and added these, together with the additional likely 20 immediate family groups to the total number of family groups within the database (the 254 mentioned at the opening of this paper), the extended family groups only amount to 5% of family groups, or barely over 1% of all groups of accomplices in the Registers. This is a tiny proportion which would be unlikely to increase dramatically if we could identify those groups of extended family members who did not share the same surname.

Moreover, the information on the crimes committed by these family groups, as well as the offending history of group members, provides very little evidence to support the idea that criminal skills were passed between family members. Of the 198 familial groups, only 22 contained family members who had committed multiple crimes, thus having the potential to demonstrate transmission, or cause and effect (e.g. that an existing offender goes on to commit a like offence with a relation, and the latter commits further similar crimes). Few of these, if any, showed evidence of domestic instruction in crime: offending histories were often mixed and seemed unrelated to the crime undertaken in partnership, beyond the vague possibility that one family member had set a bad example for the other. It may well be that fathers schooled sons, or elder brothers instructed younger brothers, on specific criminal skills, but never committed (or were never caught committing) crime together. Moreover, there are many crimes where the need for specialist skills or some degree of pre-planning is a moot point: for example, assaults, which were often related to unpredictable events or specific circumstances, or thefts, which could be opportunistic. The possible exception to this was poaching. In the case of this crime, more than any other, we might have expected to see some evidence of instruction, especially within family groups. But given that poaching was a crime typically committed by groups of men, and poaching together would be one of the best forms of instruction in the crime, it is significant that there was only one case between 1840 and 1870 which showed any evidence that one family member potentially initiated the other. In 1846, the Jarrard brothers were convicted for poaching. The eldest, John, had two prior convictions for poaching (and was convicted again for poaching in 1847). On the other hand, the youngest, George, had no criminal record, but went on to be convicted for poaching again in 1855 (Suffolk Record Office, A609/5 ff.188, 189, A609/16 ff.260, A609/1(32) ff.230, A609/2 ff.186, A609/18 ff.18).

IV. Conclusion

Data on family life and relationships in the Ipswich Gaol Registers suggest that some revisions need to be made to our current understanding of direct instruction within the working-class home during the first half of the nineteenth century. First, as the incidence of exclusive home schooling was small, and where it did occur, the level of skill acquired was low, historians have probably overestimated the role played by the family in imparting the literate skills. Second, the Registers indicate that historians might have overlooked the occurrence and function of apprenticeships served with immediate family members, predominantly fathers. Third, the Registers confirm that instruction in criminal skills for crimes such as burglary, theft and poaching (which of all crimes were most likely to need it) was rare. Finally, the shape of the family that consistently appeared from the data in the Registers was a nuclear family. This cannot be explained away as a quirk produced by the collection of the data by the clerks, by its arrangement or cataloguing, or by the nature of the calculations on it. Adjustments made to compensate for any biases produced by these methods did not afford the extended family any greater presence. The Registers re-emphasise the importance of the nuclear family as the dominant family group against an historiography that has recently sought to re-establish the importance of kin (e.g. Raey, 1996), and point to the changing significance of that nuclear family as an educational agent.

Finally, a cautionary note. Data from the Registers tell us about those labourers and tradesmen who lived in Suffolk, and, in the majority of cases, were born in Suffolk. In fact, because so many of the offenders were born in Suffolk (75%), performing the same queries as above on these offenders only made no difference to the results. Conversely, the range of birth places of those not born in Suffolk generated variable results which were difficult to interpret with certainty. As early as 1972, Michael Anderson warned researchers of family life to beware of local peculiarities which prevent national generalisations being made from regional statistics (Anderson, 1972). It may well be that conditions in Suffolk encouraged sons to establish their own, separate homes, hence increasing the importance of the nuclear family *in this county*. Similarly, in his study of mid-century Suffolk, John Glyde drew attention to the large number of labourers' wives who were employed in field work. Glyde wrote that the consequence of this was the destruction of home comforts and the transformation of the labourer's cottage into a night shelter for family members (Glyde, 1856). The practical consequence might have been that in Suffolk both parents had little time for instructing their children in the literate skills. Thus, more than anything, the Ipswich Gaol Registers show that more research is needed on the domestic curriculum.

Acknowledgements

Research for this article was made possible by the generous assistance of the Marc Fitch Fund. I am also grateful for the insights and suggestions from Christina de Bellaigue and the anonymous referee during the preparation of the text.

Disclosure statement

No potential conflict of interest was reported by the author.

References

Anderson, M. A. (1972). The study of family structure. In E. A. Wrigley (Ed.), *Nineteenth-century society: Quantitative methods for the study of social data* (pp. 47–81). Cambridge: Cambridge University Press.

Berkshire Record Office (BRO). Quarter Sessions, Q/SO 20, Annual Report of the Chaplain at Reading Gaol, 13 October 1845; Q/SO 24 & 25: Reports of the Chaplain to the Michaelmas Quarter Sessions, 1854–1857.

Browning, C. A. (1847). *The convict ship, and England's exiles: In two parts.* London: Hamilton Adams.

Crone, R. (2010). Reappraising Victorian literacy through prison records. *Journal of Victorian Culture, 15*, 3–37.

Cullen, M. J. (1975). *The statistical movement in early Victorian Britain: The foundations of empirical social research.* Hassocks: Harvester Press.

Davis, J. (1989). Jennings buildings and the royal borough: The construction of an underclass in mid-Victorian England. In D. Feldman & G. S. Jones (Eds.), *Metropolis London: Histories and representations since 1800* (pp. 11–39). London: Routledge.

Digest of parochial returns made to the Select Committee on Education of the Poor (1818), Volumes I, II, III. (Parliamentary Papers, 1819, IX-A, IX-B, IX-C).

Dobraszczyk, P. (2009). 'Give in your account': Using and abusing Victorian census forms. *Journal of Victorian Culture, 14*, 1–25.

Education enquiry: Abstract of the answers and returns on state of education in England and Wales, 1833, Volumes I, II, III. (Parliamentary Papers, 1835, XLI, XLIII, XLII).

Fletcher, J. (1843). Progress of crime in the United Kingdom. *Journal of the Statistical Society of London, 6*, 218–240.

Fletcher, J. (1847). Moral and educational statistics of England and Wales. *Journal of the Statistical Society of London, 10*, 193–233.

Fletcher, J. (1849). Moral and educational statistics of England and Wales. *Journal of the Statistical Society of London, 12*, 151–176, 189–335.

Gatrell, V. A. C. (1989). Crime, authority and the policeman-state. In F. M. L. Thompson (Ed.), *Cambridge social history of Britain, III* (pp. 241–310). Cambridge: Cambridge University Press.

Glyde, J. (1856). *Suffolk in the nineteenth century: Physical, social, moral, religious and industrial.* London: Simpkin, Marshall & Co.

Godfrey, B. S., Cox, D. J., & Farrall, S. D. (2007). *Criminal lives: Family life, employment and offending.* Oxford: Oxford University Press.

Godfrey, B. S., & Lawrence, P. (2005). *Crime and justice, 1750–1950.* Cullompton: Willan.

Griffin, E. (2013). *Liberty's dawn: A people's history of the industrial revolution.* New Haven: Yale University Press.

Hay, D. (1975). Poaching and the game laws on Cannock Chase. In D. Hay, P. Linebaugh, J. Rule, E. P. Thompson, & C. Winslow (Eds.), *Albion's fatal tree: Crime and society in eighteenth-century England* (pp. 189–253). New York: Pantheon.

Humphries, J. (2010). *Childhood and child labour in the British industrial revolution*. Cambridge: Cambridge University Press.

Joseph, H. S. (1853). *Memoirs of convicted prisoners, accompanied by remarks on the causes and prevention of crime*. London: Wertheim.

Kingsmill, J. D. (1854). *Chapters on prisons and prisoners, and the prevention of crime*. London: Longman.

Lane, J. (1996). *Apprenticeship in England, 1600–1914*. London: UCL Press.

Levine, D. (1979). Education and family life in early industrial England. *Journal of Family History, 4,* 368–380.

Mayhew, H., & Binny, J. (1862). *The criminal prisons of London and scenes of prison life*. London: Griffin, Bohn & Company.

Mitch, D. F. (1992). *The rise of popular literacy in Victorian England: The influence of private choice and public policy*. Philadelphia: University of Pennsylvania Press.

Nicholas, S. J. (1990). Literacy and the industrial revolution. In G. Tortella (Ed.), *Education and Economic development since the industrial revolution* (pp. 47–68). Valencia: Generalitat Valenciana.

Osborne, H., & Winstanley, M. (2006). Rural and urban poaching in Victorian England. *Rural History, 17,* 187–212.

Porter, G. R. (1837). On the connexion between crime and ignorance as exhibited in the criminal calendars. *Transactions of the Statistical Society, 1,* 97–103.

Raey, B. (1991). The context and meaning of popular literacy: Some evidence from nineteenth-century rural England. *Past & Present, 131,* 89–129.

Raey, B. (1996). Kinship and neighbourhood in nineteenth-century rural England: The myth of the autonomous nuclear family. *Journal of Family History, 21,* 87–104.

Rawson, R. W. (1841). An enquiry into the condition of criminal offenders in England and Wales with respect to education. *Journal of the Statistical Society of London, 3,* 331–352.

Select Committee on the Police of the Metropolis. (Parliamentary Papers, 1828, VI).

Shore, H. (1999). *Artful dodgers: Youth and crime in early nineteenth-century London*. Woodbridge: Boydell & Brewer.

Snell, K. D. M. (1985). *Annals of the labouring poor: Social change and agrarian England, 1660–1900*. Cambridge: Cambridge University Press.

Suffolk Record Office (Ipswich). Ipswich County Gaol Receiving Registers, A609/1–A609/30 (1840–1870).

The National Archives (TNA). ADM101/13/9, Medical journal of the convict ship Buffalo by J M Hamilton, Assistant Surgeon [1833]; ADM101/16/2, Medical journal of HM convict ship Captain Cook, from 4 April to 10 September 1833 by John Morgan, surgeon and superintendent; MT32/2, Journal of Mr William Crawford, Lincelles Convict Ship, 7 September 1861 to 30 January 1862.

Vincent, D. (1983). Reading in the working-class home. In J. K. Walton, & J. Walvin (Eds.), *Leisure in Britain, 1780–1939* (pp. 208–226). Manchester: Manchester University Press.

Vincent, D. (1989). *Literacy and popular culture: England, 1780–1914*. Cambridge: Cambridge University Press.

Wiener, M. J. (1990). *Reconstructing the criminal: Culture, law and policy in England, 1830–1914*. Cambridge: Cambridge University Press.

Wood, J. C. (2004). *Violence and crime in nineteenth-century England: The shadow of our refinement*. London: Routledge.

Charlotte Mason, home education and the Parents' National Educational Union in the late nineteenth century

Christina de Bellaigue
Exeter College, Oxford, UK

This article examines the work of educationist Charlotte Mason (1842–1923) to explore the practice of home education in the late nineteenth century. Mason's work reflected and responded to the particular circumstances and concerns of her clientele. She provided a way for parents to compensate for the practical deficiencies of contemporary educational provision, while engaging with current pedagogical theory. In the process, she demonstrated the enduring appeal of a strand of pedagogical thought resistant to the dominant educational models, but not hostile to institutional education per se.

Charlotte Mason (1842–1923) is today best known in the United States. There, she is cited as an inspiration for the home-schooling movement (Andreola, 1998; Levison, 2000). In Britain, by contrast, she has largely been forgotten, and is neglected by historians of education concerned with institutions and policy. At the time of her death in 1923, however, Mason was considered by *The Times* to have had a 'personal influence probably more widespread than that of any educationist of her time' (Obituary, *The Times*, 17 January 1923, p. 13). In her numerous publications—including *Home Education* (1886)—and through the Parents' National Educational Union (PNEU), she developed an educational philosophy which proved popular in late nineteenth-century Britain. In the early twentieth century, her approach was disseminated more widely as families throughout the British Empire took up her correspondence course, and as Mason's ideas were adopted in private schools and even in some maintained elementary schools (Behlmer, 1998, p. 159).

Mason's work has received some scholarly attention. Stephanie Spencer argues that Mason was ahead of her time in developing a liberal curriculum that was to be offered to boys and girls, irrespective of class, in a period when educational provision was highly class- and gender-specific (Spencer, 2010). Other scholars have focused more on the PNEU (Behlmer, 1998; Musgrove, 1959; Woodley, 2009). Behlmer and Woodley emphasise the way that the PNEU sought to respond to contemporary parental concerns. However there has been no sustained analysis of the reasons why Mason and the PNEU appealed so widely and to whom. This article seeks to fill that gap. It is based on the analysis of Mason's early work, on articles in the journal of the PNEU between 1890 and 1900, and on the papers preserved in the Charlotte Mason Archive in the Armitt Library. It sets Mason's ideas in context and examines the social origins and motivations of those who followed her in the period 1886–1900 when the PNEU was being established (after which its focus shifted more towards the Empire and towards promoting Mason's ideas for adoption in schools). In the process, this article sheds light on the practice of home education at a time when institutional education was increasingly considered essential. It argues that while Mason represented her work as modern, she also drew on long-established traditions of advice literature and educational writing. At the same time, it demonstrates that contextualising Mason's thought and practice reveals the extent to which it developed specifically in response to the educational landscape of late nineteenth-century England rather than as a philosophy of home education.

I. Charlotte Mason, *Home Education* and the origins of the PNEU

Little is known about Charlotte Mason's early life. What we do know, however, situates her firmly within the movement to develop teacher training. Born in 1842, in 1860, she enrolled at the Home and Colonial School Society (HCSS) Training College in London (Cholmondely, 1960, p. 6). This establishment trained teachers, mainly for elementary schools, along Pestalozzian and Froebelian lines (emphasising child-centred approaches to teaching and learning) and was an important influence on many of the key figures in women's education (Bellaigue, 2007, Ch. 2). From there, she became the head mistress of an infant school, and then joined a teacher-training college in Chichester as lecturer in hygiene and physiology and tutor in practical pedagogy. In 1878, however, a serious breakdown led to her moving to live with a schoolmistress friend in Bradford. There, in 1885–1886, she gave a series of lectures on the role of parents in education. Her lectures were published as *Home Education: A Course of Lectures to Ladies* in 1886. As this chronology makes clear, it was in her capacity as a professional educator, and trainer of teachers, that she addressed the 'Ladies' in her title.

In the first edition of *Home Education*, Mason set out her key ideas on the role of parents—and more particularly mothers—in the nurture and instruction of children. She drew inspiration from current psychological theory, reflecting a contemporary interest in scientific approaches to children's development that would lead to the emergence of the Child Study movement in the 1890s (Behlmer, 1998, pp. 136–146; Shuttleworth, 2010, Ch. 14). Citing William Carpenter's *Principles of Mental Physiology* (1874) and the work of Herbert Spencer, amongst others, Mason argued that parents needed to understand child physiology and psychology if they hoped to educate their offspring effectively. This she presented as a self-consciously modern approach: 'Hitherto' she argued, 'children have been brought up upon traditional methods mainly', but in the wake of the new science 'the traditions of the elders have been tried and found wanting' (Mason, 1886, pp. 2–4). Now, mothers must master a 'science of education' and direct the instruction of their children accordingly. The principle means advocated by Mason in this process were 'atmosphere', 'living ideas' and the cultivation of habit. By 'atmosphere' she meant that children should be exposed to a wide range of influences. Her notion of 'living ideas' (and 'living books') was that young people should be offered a generous curriculum which drew on the best of literature and thought, rather than being tailored specifically to children, again referring to contemporary theories of mind to explain her strategies (Mason, 1886, pp. 131, 127). Her final emphasis was on the importance of cultivating habits to counter 'that weakness of will which is the bane of most of us', and here once more, she referred to contemporary science to underline the importance of early training and habit formation: 'the actual conformation of the child's brain depends upon the habits which the parents permit or encourage' (Mason, 1886, pp. 70, 84). In *Home Education* then, Mason developed a conception of education, and specific pedagogical strategies, which highlighted the important role mothers and fathers should play in their children's development. These she presented as derived from new scientific theories of mental growth.

Significantly, *Home Education* was not a manifesto for domestic instruction. While Mason asserted that education in the home was almost always preferable for younger children, she did not recommend home education for older children: after the age of nine, 'the discipline of the school is so valuable that the boy or girl who grows up without it is at a disadvantage through life' (Mason, 1886, p. 214). The last part of *Home Education* then, advises parents on how to support children at school, and how to support girls after school.[1] It is written with the confidence of a professional who had expert knowledge of contemporary educational practice, and with a sympathetic understanding of the situation of young middle-class women who, living with their parents while waiting for marriage 'want scope, and … the discipline of work' (Mason, 1886, pp. 203–207, 276). Presenting her approach as distinctively adapted to the modern age, she set out her vision of the ways in which advanced and educated mothers should provide for their children's physical and intellectual growth, and for their moral development. They would do so first through the home schoolroom, and then by acting as auxiliaries to trained schoolteachers.

For all her emphasis on the 'modern' character of her strategies, Mason was writing in a long tradition of advice literature for parents, dating back to the seventeenth century (Hilton, 2007, pp. 22–24). Even the emphasis on scientific principles was not unprecedented, with authors like Caroline Southwood Hill advising mothers in the 1840s to adopt scientific principles in caring for their children (Southwood Hill, 1865). Mason acknowledged her debt to earlier educators, referring frequently to Rousseau and the Edgeworths, and echoing their emphasis on the value of allowing children to learn for themselves from nature (Mason, 1886, pp. 107, 151; *Parents' Review* [hereafter *PR*], I, 1890, p. 514) and frequently evoking a pastoral idyll as the ideal location for children's learning. At the same time, she offered very practical advice. *Home Education* included detailed instructions on meals and nursery furniture and drew analogies between aspects of knowledge and the rituals of middle-class life. Thus, in recommending that children keep a nature diary to record observations of animals and insects, she commented that 'there is hardly a day when some friend may not be expected to hold a first "At Home"' (referring to the contemporary practice of regularly being 'at home' to receive visitors) (Mason, 1886, p. 41). Her writing exemplifies the hybrid character of many treatises of this period—blending science, literary allusions and analogies with daily life: writing in a way that evoked a long-standing pastoral tradition of progressive education, Mason developed an educational philosophy with considerable contemporary appeal. *Home Education* was generally well received and favourably reviewed in *The Scotsman* and the *Manchester Guardian*, and *The Academy*, which emphasised its reasonable and sensible approach (Spencer, 2010, p. 117; Woodley, 2009, p. 269). A second edition was published in 1896.

The most significant impact of *Home Education*, however, was in galvanising support for the PNEU. This began in Bradford when, 'a few persons met in a neighbouring drawing room to discuss a scheme for a Parents' Educational Union' whose purpose was to educate parents as to 'the Laws of Education' (*PR*, I, 1890, pp. 69–70). In 1890, the first volume of the association's monthly periodical—the *Parents' Review*— appeared. Mason, who had moved to Ambleside in the Lake District in 1891, and set up the headquarters of the PNEU there, was the editor. In 1892, apparently prompted by parental demand, Mason set up the Parents' Review School (PRS), an innovative correspondence course which provided specially tailored curricula and schedules to families, with examination papers at the end of each term. It was aimed principally at children under the age of nine, but also catered for 'girls of the professional class, living in the country' and 'girls of the highest class' who were not always sent to school (*PR*, II, 1892, pp. 308–317). In the same year, the association adopted a federal structure and declared themselves a national body—the Parents' National Educational Union (PNEU). By 1897, the PNEU counted 31 branches nationwide with a total of 1615 members and the prospect of new branches being established in Belgium, India and South Africa. Local branches organised lectures on education and nurture for parents, brought children together for specialised teaching, and provided various resources (*PNEU Report*, 1897).

If Mason underlined the domestic, drawing-room origins of the PNEU, she also continued to argue that those caring for children needed training, and in 1892 she embarked on two ventures intended to professionalise the care and teaching of children in the home. The first was the Mothers' Education Course (MEC) intended to encourage women to prepare themselves more effectively for supervising their own children's education. It ran until 1915. The second was the House of

Education in Ambleside, which offered a year's training and was aimed at 'earnest and well-bred women who are looking out for good work' usually as governesses (*PNEU Report*, 1897, p. 53). By 1897, it had trained 85 young women and was being recommended in periodicals like the *Monthly Packet*, a journal aimed at young middle-class women (Green (1895)), and to mothers in search of governesses through journals like *Hearth and Home: An Illustrated Weekly Journal for Gentlewomen* ('Answers to correspondents', 1900).

The fact that Mason's activities centred on Ambleside was significant. There, she was in close contact with Selina Fleming—a friend from the HCSS Training College. Fleming had taken over a school previously established in Ambleside by Anne Jemima Clough, the first principal of Newnham College, Cambridge. Clough also had connections to the HCSS, and supported teacher training, and Mason consulted her on how best to manage the PNEU (*PR*, VIII, 1897, p. 51; Sutherland, 2006, p. 47). While supporting education in the home, Mason thus shored up her connections to the movement to develop teaching as a profession, situating herself within a cluster of forward-thinking educators. Indeed, in all her ventures, Mason cultivated and was supported by a growing network of very able teachers and parents and made good use of her contacts with some of the key contemporary figures in education. Emily Shirreff (co-founder of the Girls Public Day School Trust and leading Froebelian), Michael Sadler (later Director of the Board of Education) and Oscar Browning (principal of the Cambridge Day Training College) amongst others, all contributed to the *Parents' Review* and participated in the formation of the Union. By the mid 1890s, the PNEU was established as a forum where key figures in education might share their ideas with a growing group of active and interested parents.

As this rapid overview reveals, Mason was a successful educational entrepreneur as well as an educational philosopher. By comparison with other contemporary educational organisations, the PNEU was not large. In the 1890s, the University Extension Movement was attracting in the region of 20,000 students; by 1906, there were 13,052 members of the National Home Reading Union (Goldman, 1995, p. 61; Snape, 2002, p. 103). In the 1900s, the PNEU gained strength particularly in the colonies (a subject which requires further research[2]), but in the 1890s, its membership was not huge and its ambitions were more limited. Yet Mason was effective in her efforts to recruit, and by 1899, 80 women had enrolled on the MEC (Kitching, 1923, p. 139); in 1900, there were about 300 families registered for the PRS (Woodley, 2009, p. 253). By 1907, there were 2300 subscribers to the *Parents' Review* and by 1913, the central office of the PNEU was processing between 12,000 and 13,000 letters per year (*PNEU Report*, 1907, p. 15, 1913, p. 19). Mason and the PNEU were also attracting attention more widely. The establishment of the PNEU was reported in the national press (not always favourably—*Macmillan's Magazine* ran a critical piece describing it as a demanding and unnecessary intrusion into the life of the 'poor breadwinner' ('Cry of the parents', 1890). Local branch meetings and lectures were covered in the regional papers, and Mason used articles in the national press to publicise and develop her ideas

(Spencer, 2010, p. 109). What this press interest, the growing numbers of participants in Mason's various programmes, as well as the rapid dissemination of her ideas suggest is that she was answering needs widely felt. Through the correspondence course, the lectures and services provided by the PNEU branches, the MEC, the House of Education, Mason was influencing the work of parents in 'home-schoolrooms' nationwide.

II. The 'children of educated people': the clientele of the PNEU

In the period between 1887 and 1900, the families joining the PNEU were largely drawn from established land-holding families, professional families and the upper middle class more widely, while there was also a steady stream of members from lower down the social scale. This recruitment pattern is partly explained by the contemporary institutional context.

Formal schooling was on the rise. In the second half of the nineteenth century institutional provision for the education of children and adolescents steadily expanded. From the 1870s, new legislation led to the gradual emergence of a national system of free schools. These, however, were elementary schools, intended for the working class, and catering for children between the ages of 5 and 10. A range of secondary schools catered for better-off children between the ages of 8 and 18. These too were expanding their provision and numbers; but this very expansion threw into relief the need to provide for the earlier education of middle- and upper-class children, whose parents would not contemplate sending them anywhere near elementary schools (Sutherland, 1990, pp. 141–152). Private 'preparatory' schools, aimed at such younger children, had been growing in number since the beginning of the century, but were still only available to a minority (Leinster-Mackay, 1975). By offering a structured programme for the education of younger children at home the PNEU was filling an obvious gap in the middle- and upper-class market.

Simultaneously and paradoxically the expansion of formal school provision for elite children was enhancing the importance of home provision, enabling it to be seen as complementary in crucial ways. It could ensure that children were well-prepared for entry into an institutional framework after the age of eight. It could also run in parallel with an intermittent sampling of institutional provision, much more marked for girls than for boys. In the 1850s the average stay of boys at one school was just 2.6 years (Roach, 1986, p. 62). Of a sample of 44 middle-class girls born between 1800 and 1860, 43% spent fewer than four years at school (Bellaigue, 2007, p. 139).

This was beginning to change in the second half of the nineteenth century, but slowly and unevenly. Already in 1868, 98% of the 2403 students—all male—then at Oxford and Cambridge had spent more than two years in school (Woodley, 2009, p. 260). In a study of 131 elite families by Mark Rothery (2009), 67% of sons of the cohort of 61 born during 1880–1889 had been sent to school, yet 60% of the daughters in his 131 families, and 33% of the 1880–1889 cohort of boys, were being educated entirely at home. Similarly, Janet Howarth found that in the early 1880s, 15% of the students at the new Oxbridge colleges for women had been educated at home or 'privately' (Howarth, 1985, p. 62).

Even in the last decades of the century, institutional schooling was far from universal in elite families, especially for daughters; and encounters with it might form only one part of a diverse and varied educational itinerary. But this increasingly high profile of institutional instruction underpinned the appeal of Charlotte Mason's work. The PNEU and its associated activities offered a way of ensuring that middle-class and elite children educated at home in part or in whole need not be at a disadvantage in relation to those taught in school. In the context of the class-stratified expansion of institutional instruction and growing educational competition, an organisation offering guidance on the management of home learning and instruction could thrive. These growths were inter-twined.

Mason herself initially clearly assumed and sought to target an audience with a degree of economic security; she also frequently aimed her writing explicitly at women (see below). Thus, she expected that her 'lady' readers would have a governess, and with any luck, a trained governess, to work with. She assumed that the families she was working with were part of 'Society'. In 1890, a meeting of the executive committee of the PNEU was delayed till October, so that it would be convenient for families 'returning to town for the Winter Season' (*PR*, I, 1890, p. 639). She also made much of her patrons among the landed gentry and aristocracy. The Countess of Aberdeen became president of the society in 1892, and titled new members were made vice-presidents of the Union (*PNEU Report*, 1897, p. 2). This was good publicity, and may have been part of a strategy intended to appeal to parents with social aspirations, but it did also reflect a significant audience for the society, judging by the registers of the MEC for 1892–1907, and indeed Lady Aberdeen was a very active and engaged member of the Union (AL, CM 22, Mothers Education Course, 1892–1907). Of the 120 women who took the course between 1892 and 1907, a sample of 27 have been traced in civil records. Of these, four were the wives of peers or upper gentry, four were married to large-scale businessmen and manufacturers (ship-owners, textile manufacturers) and three were married to high-ranking military officers. Only three had husbands in lower status white-collar occupations. Many had homes in London and in the countryside (as would be expected if they followed the Season), and they had an average of 3.5 live-in servants. Eight had resident governesses, and 15 had a resident nurse. These were clearly women of considerable means and social standing.

However, the PNEU was also attracting attention lower down the social scale. The MEC correspondence, and letters to the *Parents' Review*, reveal a steady flow of members from provincial cities and rural areas, who clearly struggled to keep up with the work that the course involved whilst juggling many other responsibilities. In about 1903, Ethel T. Matthews wrote from a vicarage in Monmouthshire to say that she could not take the MEC exam. She wrote:

> I think you will realise a little of my difficulty when I tell you I have 3 little children the eldest 4, the baby 16 months. I have only a young nurse—which means a great deal of the care of the children falls to me—then after I have done their sewing of an Evening—or when I can fit it in—so many [tasks] for the vicarage ... & one finds no spare time to oneself. (AL, PNEU II/29/38, Matthews to Mason, nd. [c.1903?])

Similarly, in the first issue of the *Review* a letter from 'Mater', the mother of four children aged between one and seven asked 'how is a mother to fulfill her duties?'. She described her day in detail, recording her many activities—arranging meals, dusting, teaching the children in the mornings, making them practise their instruments, making sure they took their afternoon walk, putting the babies to bed, making the children's clothes, as well as her need to 'keep abreast of the times', and 'social duties' (*PR*, I, 1890, p. 77). The letter indicates how home education in this period need not imply informality or lack of regime, and also suggests the pressures that this might put on some mothers. Responses to 'Mater' from other parents in the next issue suggested early rising, employing a very cheap seamstress, and better self-government. Such letters indicate a wider audience for the PNEU than Mason's references to 'the Season' suggest. These readers were not impoverished, but they had to manage a middle-class family and middle-class cultural aspirations on a limited income and in circumstances unlike those of the wives of peers who also appeared in the MEC registers.

The large number of clergymen and missionary wives among the correspondents of the *Parents' Review* and those enrolled on the MEC raises the question of religious background. Mason herself seems to have been from a Quaker background—interesting given the Quaker tradition of parents providing a 'guarded education' at home for their children, in order to preserve the purity of Quakerism (Leach, 2002, p. 49). In adulthood, however, she emphasised spirituality and reverence, rather than specific beliefs (Spencer, 2010, p. 110). And while she stressed the importance of religious education for children and cultivating their sense of the spiritual, what she advocated was non-denominational; she was critical of 'believing parents' who relied only on the Bible for guidance, arguing that the sciences of education were also the 'laws of God' and must be studied (Mason, 1886, pp. 27–29). This meant that her ideas might have inter-denominational and even inter-faith appeal. While the elite members of the PNEU were likely to have been members of the Church of England and the Vice-Presidents of the society included many prominent Anglican bishops, one of the most dynamic organising secretaries—Henrietta Franklin—was from a prominent Jewish family and a notable advocate of Liberal Judaism. The PNEU thus not only recruited across a wide social range, it recruited across religious divides.

Mason's emphasis on education and expertise helped the PNEU to draw together this rather socially disparate group of parents. While she sometimes played up 'Society' connections, she more often described those she was seeking to provide for as 'the children of educated parents'. In the longer term, this way of constituting the community allowed Mason to broaden the appeal and reach of the PNEU, since it was increasingly the case that it was not only the parents of the middle and upper classes who might be described as 'educated'. In the 1890s, however, this language was specifically intended to appeal to those in the middle and upper classes and the *Parents' Review* was represented by Mason as a publication addressed to an educated elite, noting that 'it is not what is called "popular literature", and does not appeal to the many' (*PR*, March 1892, p. 77). The language of education, expertise and exclusive sophistication was central to the appeal of the PNEU.

Significant too, was the focus on mothers and the 'ladies' addressed in the full title of *Home Education*. While the *Parents' Review* was explicitly dedicated to parents rather than mothers, and fathers represented a fair proportion of its correspondents, as well as being permitted to join the PNEU, in Mason's account of the origins of the Union she records that it had been agreed only 'after protest' that fathers should be allowed to join (*PR*, II, 1890, pp. 69–70). We have no knowledge of who made this protest or on what grounds, but it is clear that Mason—at certain times—did have a specifically female audience in mind. Thus, in *Home Education*, Mason explicitly couched her advice as responding to the needs of women, who, as they became more educated, also became more aware of their responsibilities as mothers. She predicted that in the process, mothers would take up child-rearing 'as their profession—that is, with the diligence, regularity, and punctuality which men bestow on their professional labours' (Mason, 1886, p. 2) (the parallel with medicine, the law and other male professions providing another indication of the social level at which her advice was pitched).

Evidence from the archives and correspondence in the *Parents' Review* suggests that this approach bore fruit, and that it was principally to mothers and particularly to those women who were benefiting from expanding opportunities for female secondary and higher education that Mason's work appealed (Holcombe, 1973, pp. 21–34). The women who joined the PNEU also shared a demographic profile. These were the mothers of families acting out wider patterns of middle- and upper-class family limitation. For elite couples marrying between 1880 and 1899, family size dropped to around 2.23 children, though there were regional variations in the patterns of decline (Rothery, 2009, p. 677). Similarly, in the 72 families enrolled on the PRS in 1891, the average family size was 2.2 children (Woodley, 2009, p. 278). For the 27 women in the MEC registers sample, the average number of children was slightly larger at 3.1, but well down on the average of 4.5 children born to landowners' families for the cohorts marrying between 1825 and 1849 (Rothery, 2009, p. 679). At the same time (and not unrelated), the mothers enrolled on the MEC seem to be women who were starting their families relatively late, with an average age of 30 at the birth of their first living child. It may be that, as older mothers they were less able to draw on the expertise of the previous generation, and were particularly attracted by the advice that the PNEU might offer. Whatever the truth of this, these figures suggest that the PNEU was attracting women of a certain social status whose work as parents was focused on a limited number of children.

These older mothers were also women who might have had several years of independent activity, even professional experience (see Holcombe (1973) on the expanding range of careers open to middle- and upper-class women in this period). Mason had written with particular sympathy of the situation of young women living at home and of their need for serious activity. Her work might well be expected to resonate particularly with women who saw Mason's approach as supportive of an active and engaged life for educated women before and after marriage, and it does seem that several of those enrolled on the MEC had pursued further education and their own careers before marrying. For example, in 1898, Agnes Kinnear wrote from Dundee to enquire about the course noting that she had a BA from the University of London and taught for three years before her marriage (Kinnear to Mason, 17 November 1898, AL, PNEU II, AL, PNEU II/29). Such women were like those identified by Sian Pooley, who aspired to a wider variety of roles than their mothers and whose desire to preserve their independent activities influenced fertility strategies among elite families (Pooley, 2013, p. 91). In this context, it seems relevant that both the letters from Matthews and 'Mater' quoted above refer to a desire for 'time for oneself', a theme that was also the subject of numerous letters to the *Parents' Review*, prompting mothers to write in with advice on how to ensure that their time would not be interrupted (*PR*, I, 1890, p. 225). The families of the PNEU were headed by a new generation of educated women, who both expected to devote considerable time and energy to their children, but also considered their own time as valuable. The PNEU appealed to their sense of themselves as 'professional' mothers, expert in the raising of children, but also answered a need reinforced by the expansion of female education, for some personal autonomy.

In the years up to 1900 the PNEU brought together middle- and upper-class families seeking to provide for the education of their children in the context of a class-stratified institutional framework. While a significant minority of elite children received the entirety of their education in the home, the number of middle-class and gentry families who expected to send their children to school for at least part of the time was growing. Mothers of markedly different levels of wealth, but with a similar sense of distance from the working class, with similar family structures, and a similar belief in the importance of their work as mothers, were united by their desire for support in the instruction of their children in a period when institutional education had yet to become universal but was already setting the agenda.

III. 'The hurry of the age': the appeal of the PNEU

Mason's emphasis on educational qualifications and professionalism of mothers was echoed by her belief in the notion of parenthood as requiring training. Using the language of profession to characterise motherhood was nothing new. It had been a common theme in advice literature since the end of the eighteenth century (Bellaigue, 2007, p. 15). As we have seen, earlier authors had also advocated adopting a scientific approach to child-rearing. What was distinctive, however, was her insistence on training, and particularly scientific training. This was one way in which Mason emphasised the modernity of her 'new departure', and tapped into the contemporary currents of thought of the child study movement (Shuttleworth, 2010).

The PNEU clearly situated itself within this movement, and responded in part to parental demand for more knowledge and understanding of the new sciences of childhood. Local branches organised lectures on 'The psychology of attention' and 'The anatomy and physiology of the skin in relation to children's clothing' (*PNEU Report*, 1897, pp. 20, 26) and the *Parents' Review* explicitly presented itself as an organ which would disseminate such expertise. In the first 10 years of its existence it published at least 16 articles on hygiene, alongside articles on the psychology of children in the nursery, discussions of diet, physical exercise and the scientific principles on which the curriculum should be designed. Many members saw themselves as improving on the approach taken by earlier generations (*PR*, VII, p. 26). Indeed, the push by women to redefine motherhood and parenting in the second half of the nineteenth century may partly have reflected a general sense that their own experiences were unsatisfactory (Peterson, 1998, p. 107).

The MEC provides further evidence of the desire for scientific approaches to parenthood, and particularly motherhood, since scientific study was a key part of the hefty programme of reading and examination it involved. Undertaken over three years, the course required reading about 100 pages a week for 10 months each year, followed by a stiff examination. Many subscribers failed to complete their examinations, yet the registers do record a steady stream of mothers receiving favourable comments on their papers (AL, CM 22 'Mothers Education Course, 1891–1900, 143). There was evidently considerable appetite among mothers of this generation for the kind of professionalised training for parenthood that Mason offered.

This demand for advice and training might also be fuelled by the anxieties that awareness of the new sciences of childhood might foster. One of the most frequently recurring themes of mothers' letters, evident in the letters already cited, is a concern about the demands of domestic life, and the letter-writer's lack of time, expertise or ability to provide adequately professional parenting. Thus, in 1890, EAD wrote to the *Parents' Review* asking for Mason to consider setting out a scheme of education to help mothers plan schoolroom life. Such a scheme, she argued:

> would very much help many a young mother who has to buy her experience at the cost of many failures, through ignorance. We want a little practical instruction as to how best to map out the day—so as to give the children the best advantages for their growing bodies—combined with minds so well furnished that they will be able, having been thoroughly and correctly grounded, to take a good place at school. (*PR*, I, p. 318)

These were mothers who were deeply aware of the new ideas circulating about education in society, and also of the importance of preparing their children to succeed in school, but who felt inadequate to the task. Such anxieties and concerns reflected in miniature a broader sense of uncertainty articulated by many contributors to the *Review* and by many of Mason's correspondents, and which shaped a major concern of the PNEU—the relationship between home and school.

As noted above, Mason was explicit in her preference for school instruction for older children. Her intention for the home-schoolroom in fact, was explicitly intended to mitigate the dangers of home education. These she identified as precocity, dilettantism and what would now be understood as a failure to fully socialise the child (*PR*, III, p. 279). Significantly, Mason believed readers would share her perspective on the value of schooling. Thus, in 1893 for example, she sought to reassure 'those parents who regret deeply their inability to send their children to school that our experience in connection with the PRS tends to show that the average home-taught child may keep well abreast of the school-taught child' (*PR*, III, p. 279). The clear assumption here was that parents would prefer to send their children to school. Evidence from the PRS correspondence course and from the MEC correspondence suggests that this was indeed the case, and that the correspondence school was used principally for the education of younger children. Thus of 160 children enrolled in the course in 1891, the average age of the boys was around eight, and for girls it was around nine (Woodley, 2009, p. 278). Similarly, at the point at which mothers in the MEC sample joined, the average age of their eldest child was 4.3. The correspondence suggests that the decision to do so was sometimes partly prompted by the inadequacy or inaccessibility of the schools available to them (AL, PNEU II/29 F. Sharp to C. Mason, 19 July 1897). For all the evidence of significant numbers of elite children being educated at home, the dominant force in education was assumed to be the school.

Yet many articles and letters in the *Review* reveal that the relationship between home education and school instruction, and between parents and teachers, could be tense and anxious. These relations were thus the subject of at least 20 articles between 1890 and 1900, and 'harmonising home and school training' was one of the stated objects of the Union. That parents and home education were on the back foot, however, is apparent from the repeated emphasis that a home-educated child, if properly trained, would not fall behind a child sent to a kindergarten or secondary school, or even the working-class children in elementary schools. While Mason and the PNEU sought to support parents in the education of their children, it was schools that were setting the agenda. The *Parents' Review* provided an arena for parents to negotiate this new relationship but did not fundamentally challenge the growing dominance of institutional education.

Anxiety about how best to prepare children for school, and which schools to choose, reflected a more general sense of uncertainty about prospects for middle-class children. Thus, in September 1890, one mother wrote to 'Notes and Queries' to ask for advice on the best books for little boys, commenting that 'teachers in National Schools have their lines laid down most clearly step by step, but we are left to pick up wisdom as we can' (*PR*, I, p. 557). The 'National Schools' she referred to were those publicly-funded elementary schools for the working class which were, by then, chiefly staffed by teachers who had received at least some training.[3] Her comment hints not only at a sense of inadequacy in the face of professional teachers, but also at a sense of social competition, not only with other middle-class families, but also with the working classes who now benefitted from such instruction.

This sense that elite children might face new challenges, and anxiety about the future, was apparent in other letters. It also explains the series of articles in the *Parents' Review* between 1890 and 1900 on the subject of 'Our Sons' or 'Our Daughters', providing detailed information about careers in the navy, the law and journalism for boys, and in education for girls. These articles explained to parents how to ensure their child's success in each field, and gave details of the cost of training and the likely rewards in relation to the investment required. Articles like this, and the emphasis on the need to keep up with children in schools, particularly working-class children, reflected the impact of social changes in the late nineteenth century which were undermining the traditional dominance of the landed elites. The family limitation strategies adopted by middle-class and gentry families in the 1880s and 1890s were, in part, a response to the contemporary reduction of incomes and the collapse of aristocratic wealth as a result of the declining value of land (Rothery, 2009, p. 683). In the context of increasing professionalisation, elite and families were newly conscious of the need to provide for their children's education and training (Perkin, 1989; Cannadine, 1990, Ch. 5). The PNEU and *Parents' Review* seemed to provide a way for middle-class and elite parents to safeguard their children's futures in a world which was increasingly competitive and challenging.

What Mason offered was a way to engage with contemporary scientific thought on childcare, whilst bolstering the authority of parents by respecting their expertise —there were 11 articles between 1890 and 1900 which claimed to be 'by a mother', echoing long-standing tropes in advice literature for parents. Older progressive pedagogical traditions also provided ways to dramatise the positive contribution that parents could make to their children's education. Articles on the Edgeworths, Froebel, Rousseau and Mrs Barbauld all emphasised the role of parents in the intellectual and moral instruction of children, and the importance of attention to the individual child. Thus, while Mason sought to distance herself from 'traditional methods' in some respects, she also drew on a long-standing tradition of progressive education, much of which emphasised informal and individual learning in the home, but which was—for the most part—not opposed to school education in itself. This was particularly evident in her relationship with Anne Jemima Clough. In Mason's eyes, Clough 'united in a unique way the old and the new. She understood and believed in parents of the sort who educated their children quietly on the lines of "Evenings at Home" etc.' (*PR*, VII, 1897, p. 51). For Mason, Clough provided a link between the modern world of trained teachers and educated women, and older traditions of parental education exemplified by *Evenings at Home* (a collection of stories by John Aikin and Anna Barbauld published between 1792 and 1796 to be read aloud; see Hilton (2007, p. 102)) which prized parents' role in the development of the individual child. In her affinity with Clough, and in the choice of the educationists she celebrated in the *Parents' Review*—Caroline Herford of the progressive Ladybarn School, Edward Thring of Uppingham—Mason was identifying herself with an educational tradition which stood somewhat apart from the dominant influences of the 'great' public schools. By referring to these educators, and indeed by holding the first London meeting of the PNEU at the headquarters of the College of Preceptors—an organisation which sought to implement some of the progressive pedagogies developed by Froebel—Mason highlighted her affinities with a strand of progressive pedagogical thinking that did not necessarily reject schooling per se (Bellaigue, 2004).

While the expansion of institutional instruction was calling into question the legitimacy of other forms of education and giving rise to parental anxieties about the need to keep up with schools, Mason and the PNEU continued to articulate a concept of education that emphasised personal influence and individual learning. They also did provide a forum for parents who called into question some of the dominant orthodoxies of late nineteenth-century education. Thus, in 1890 'IJ' responded angrily to an article by a respected teacher on punishment and discipline. It was very wrong, 'IJ' contended, to suggest that young children should be severely disciplined, and particularly criticised the notion that a child under the age of one might be branded a 'thief' for taking something they had been told not to take (*PR*, I, 1890, pp. 479–480). Similarly, in September of the same year, HD Pearsall of Orpington in Kent wrote to criticise the paper by the Headmaster of Bradford Grammar School, asserting that classical training remained 'the best curriculum'. Pearsall objected fiercely and defended the value of scientific inquiry for moral and intellectual development (*PR*, I, p. 557). Such examples demonstrate that while the elite and middle-class parents of the PNEU were increasingly expecting schools to provide instruction for their children, and anxious about competition and standards, formal provision was not being accepted uncritically.

IV. Conclusion

Charlotte Mason's work, her thinking on home education, and the organisations she established, are best understood as responses to the very particular social and intellectual context in which she was operating, rather than as a philosophy of domestic pedagogy. The contours of educational provision in the period after 1850 meant that there was a demand for the practical advice that Mason was offering. That demand was additionally fuelled by contemporary intellectual and social movements which drew attention to the role of parents in their children's education, and suggested a need for specialised and scientific training. In addition Mason articulated an educational vision which appealed to parents—and particularly to mothers—by emphasising their continued importance in cultivating their child's intellectual and cultural development, drawing on long-standing tropes in progressive pedagogical theory, as well as on new theories of psychology and physiology. The social background of the families who joined the PNEU and associated organisation, their letters in the *Parents' Review* and the Mason archives, reveal a cohort of mothers and fathers who sought actively to engage with current educational thinking and also claimed their own expertise as parents. At the same time, these parents' letters and the publications they read reflect a wider anxiety about their children's futures in a new world of educational and social competition.

In the 1910s and 1920s, Mason would work hard to extend her influence into secondary and elementary schools, focusing less on the role of parents in their children's training and more on the need for all children to receive a liberal education as 'the basis of national strength'. The Parents' Union School would thrive throughout the Empire, eventually transforming itself into the World Wide Education Service that still exists today (Spencer, 2010, p. 109). But in its early decades, the work of Charlotte Mason and the PNEU exposed the ways in which, by the end of the nineteenth century, formal institutional education was so dominant as to ensure that home education was understood as ancillary and auxiliary to what was provided in schools. At the same time, however, the experiences of the families who made up the PNEU reveal how, even then, the lines between formal and informal and institutional and home education were still blurred. They also point to the continuing appeal of a strand of progressive educational thought, not entirely aligned with the dominant educational orthodoxies, that valued the individualised and informal instruction and training that might be provided in the home.

Acknowledgements

I am grateful to Kathryn Gleadle, Gillian Sutherland, Charlotte Bennett and all the participants in the Domestic Pedagogies workshop, as well as the anonymous peer reviewers of the *ORE* for their help in developing and refining this article.

Disclosure statement

No potential conflict of interest was reported by the author.

Notes

1. She developed these subjects more fully in *Home and School Education: The Training and Education of Children Over Nine* (1905).
2. By 1907, there were four branches in Australia and branches were also set up in Ceylon (*PNEU Report*, 1907, pp. 49–51). Figures from the PNEU reports suggest that there were subscribers to the *Review* throughout the empire (*PNEU Report*, 1914, pp. 16–17). It would seem that it had a particular appeal for families who wanted to keep their children with them with the colonial branches echoing the imperial academic networks studied by Tamson Pietsch, and giving a new connotation to the understanding of 'home education' (Pietsch, 2013).
3. The correspondent was using 'National schools' as a generic term, to encompass both the new Board Schools established under the provisions of the Forster Act of 1870, and the schools provided by the Anglican Church of England.

HOME EDUCATION IN HISTORICAL PERSPECTIVE

References

Andreola, K. (1998). *A Charlotte Mason companion: Personal reflections on the gentle art of learning.* USA: Charlotte Mason Research and Supply.

'Answers to correspondents'. (1900). *Hearth & Home: An Illustrated Journal for Gentlewomen,* 459, p. 694.

Armitt Library (AL). Ambleside, Charlotte Mason Archive and papers of the PNEU (CM 22, PNEU II/29).

Behlmer, G. K. (1998). *Friends of the family: The English home and its guardians 1850–1940.* Palo Alto, CA: Stanford University Press.

Bellaigue, C. de. (2004). The development of teaching as a profession for women before 1870. *Historical Journal,* 44, 963–988.

Bellaigue, C. de. (2007). *Educating women: Schooling and identity in England and France, 1800–1870.* Oxford: Oxford University Press.

Cannadine, D. (1990). *The decline and fall of the British aristocracy.* New Haven, CT: Yale University Press.

Cholmondely, E. (1960). *The story of Charlotte Mason (1842–1923).* London: J.M. Dent.

'Cry of the parents, by one of them'. (1890, May). *Macmillan's Magazine,* pp. 55–58.

Goldman, L. (1995). *Dons and workers: Oxford and adult education since 1850.* Oxford: Oxford University Press.

Green, F. L. (1895, May 12). A house of education. *Monthly Packet* (Issue 531), p. 591.

Hilton, M. (2007). *Women and the shaping of the nation's young: Education and public doctrine in Britain 1750–1850.* Farnham: Ashgate.

Holcombe, L. (1973). *Victorian ladies at work: Middle class working women in England and Wales, 1850–1914.* Newton Abbot: David & Charles.

Howarth, J. (1985). Public schools, safety-nets and educational ladders: The classification of girls' secondary schools, 1880–1914. *Oxford Review of Education,* 11, 59–71.

Kitching, E. (1923). The beginning of things. In Charlotte M. Mason (Ed.), *In memoriam* (pp. 118–143). London: Parents' National Educational Union.

Leach, C. (2002). Advice for parents and books for children: Quaker women and educational texts for the home, 1798–1850. *History of Education Society Bulletin,* 69, 49–58.

Leinster-Mackay, D. (1975). The evolution of t'other schools: An examination of the nineteenth century development of the private preparatory school. *History of Education,* 5, 241–249.

Levison, C. (2000). *A Charlotte Mason education. A home schooling how to manual.* Beverly Hills, CA: Champion Press.

Mason, C. (1886). *Home education. Lectures to ladies.* London: Kegan Paul.

Mason, C. (1905). *Home and school education: The training and education of children over nine.* London: Kegan Paul.

Musgrove, F. (1959). Middle class families and schools 1780–1880: Interaction and exchange of functions between institutions. *Sociological Review,* 7(12), 169–178.

Obituary of Charlotte Mason. (1923, 17 January). *The Times,* p. 13.

Parents' Review. (1890–1900).

Perkin, H. (1989). *The rise of professional society. England since 1880.* London: Routledge.

Peterson, M. J. (1998). *Family, love and work in the lives of Victorian gentlewomen*. Bloomington, IN: University of Indiana Press.

Pietsch, T. (2013). *Empire of scholars: Universities, networks and the British academic world, 1850–1939*. Manchester, NH: Manchester University Press.

PNEU. (1897–1914). *Annual Reports*. London: Parents' National Educational Union.

Pooley, S. (2013). Parenthood, child-rearing and fertility in England, 1850–1914. *History of the Family, 18*, 83–106.

Roach, J. (1986). *A history of secondary education in England, 1800–1870*. London & New York: Longman.

Rothery, M. (2009). The reproductive behaviour of the English landed gentry in the nineteenth and early twentieth centuries. *Journal of British Studies, 48*, 674–694.

Shuttleworth, S. (2010). *The mind of the child: Child development in literature, science, and medicine, 1840–1900*. Oxford: Oxford University Press.

Snape, R. (2002). The National Home Reading Union. *Journal of Victorian Culture, 7*, 86–110.

Southwood Hill, C. S. (1865). *Memoranda of observations and experiments in education*. London: Vizetelly & Co.

Spencer, S. (2010). 'Knowledge as the necessary food of the mind': Charlotte Mason's philosophy of education. In J. Spence, S. J. Aiston, & M. M. Meikle (Eds.), *Women, education and agency, 1600–2000* (pp. 105–25). London: Routledge.

Sutherland, G. (1990). Education. In F. M. L. Thompson (Ed.), *The Cambridge social history of Britain 1750–1950*, Vol. III (pp. 119–170). Cambridge: Cambridge University Press.

Sutherland, G. (2006). *Faith, duty and the power of mind: The Cloughs and their circle, 1820–1960*. Cambridge: Cambridge University Press.

Woodley, S. (2009). *'Go to school they shall not': Home education and the middle classes in Britain 1760–1900* (Unpublished DPhil). Oxford: University of Oxford.

Self-education, class and gender in Edwardian Britain: women in lower middle class families

Gillian Sutherland
Newnham College, Cambridge, UK

Once societies embarked on programmes of mass education home schooling became essentially a middle-class project and remains so. This paper looks at the educational experiences of some lower middle class women at the turn of the nineteenth and twentieth centuries for whom the resources of the middle-class home were simply not available. It explores both their experiences of formal schooling and of the educational provision they chose to seek and found among other groups and institutional frameworks in their society. The range and extended chronology of their educational experiences highlight the need to reconceptualise education as extended processes of physical, intellectual and moral socialisation not necessarily limited to the years of childhood and/or adolescence or time-stopped in any way.

There has been a tendency in the historiography of the last two and a half centuries to construct a false dichotomy between formal and informal ways of learning, one which has increased in artificiality as the vogue for large schemes of mass schooling has grown in societies. This paper uses evidence about the aspirations and cultural explorations of some white-collar women workers in the Edwardian years to challenge that dichotomy. It explores relations between formal and informal modes of learning and sheds new light on notions of home education both historically and in the contemporary world. It suggests that rather than seeking to classify educational experience as either primarily formal or primarily informal, it is more helpful to see formal/informal as two poles between which many people move at different points in their lives, in search of different skills and different ideas.

By the late nineteenth century in Britain, as minimum compulsory schooling began to bite, it became increasingly difficult to find many who had had no encounter at all with formal provision—institutionalised instruction in schools—even if, as

HOME EDUCATION IN HISTORICAL PERSPECTIVE

Flora Thompson, who grew up in rural Oxfordshire, put it in her fictionalised autobiography, it 'was only the second generation to be forcibly fed with the fruit of the tree of knowledge: what wonder if it did not always agree with it' (Thompson, 1945 [1939], p. 195). Whereas in earlier periods, 'home education', instruction received in the home, might be conceptualised without reference to formal structures of educational provision, from the beginning of the twentieth century and continuing through to the beginning of the twenty-first century the ideal of home education cannot be constructed without reference to the formal structures of educational provision in the larger society: they were and are locked into perpetual dialogue. The interesting questions then become ones about the relationships between this encounter with school and other educational experiences in individual lives. Were people turned off altogether—forever or just for a time? Did the experience provide some basic tools or only occasional spurs? What else was available and how was it sought and/or delivered?

Investigating these processes further also demonstrates that other institutional frameworks besides those being developed by the state—chapels, public libraries, voluntary associations, political movements—could all have a role in individuals' educational experiences. In the effort to capture fully the range in variety, type and time-frame of the educational activities engaged in by lower middle class women in the Edwardian period, it is helpful to be reminded of Durkheim's characterisation of education as an extended process of physical, intellectual and moral socialisation, not necessarily time-stopped or limited to the years of childhood and/or adolescence (Durkheim, 1956 [1922], ch. 1).

A focus on the experiences of the lower middle class throws into relief too the class-specific ways in which home education has often been conceived. The homes of clerks and artisans seldom had either the resources or the leisure to complement or counter-balance the offerings of formal schooling in the same ways as earnest parents who subscribed to the Parents' National Education Union. None had access to the extensive private libraries drawn on by the late eighteenth-century theorists of domestic instructions and their children. The ideal of home education was and is essentially middle class. The children of late Victorian and Edwardian white-collar workers, female and male, who wanted something more and/or something different had to seek other ways and other mechanisms for finding these; the varied institutional frameworks of contemporary society were a vital, and often the only, resource. For these lower middle class and upper working class families it is more appropriate to think of self-education, rather than home education, of processes whereby individuals both sought out instruction and educational opportunities for themselves, often through these seeking also some kind of self-actualisation.

Ideas and practices of home education and self-education were not only class-specific, they were also gender-specific. Jonathan Rose has suggested that the breakthrough years for lower middle class young *women* were the years of the First World War when manpower shortages and full employment brought more and better paid work, which gave them some disposable income with which to explore cultural opportunities (Rose, 2001, pp. 412–413). There is, however, accumulating evidence to suggest that the spectacular expansion of white-collar work for women in the last third of the long nineteenth century before the outbreak of war, in particular the expansion of clerical work and of maintained school teaching, brought new opportunities for some young women to try new things—if they chose—well before the upheavals brought by war. Positions as clerks or as maintained school teachers offered new opportunities for steady, non-manual work to the daughters of the respectable working class, the labour aristocracy and the emergent lower middle class (Sutherland, 2015). Examining the educational itineraries of young lower middle class women in this period throws into high relief the novelty of what was then available, and the interaction between the formal elementary schooling, by then compulsory, and other educational experiences.

Two sets of case studies provide different versions of and insights into movements back and forth along the continuum between the poles of formal/informal. The first case study, the experiences of some women maintained school teachers, might be thought not to belong here at all; the second, the experience of some women clerks, is on the face of it, easier to accommodate. Yet both demonstrate such movements, such oscillations, albeit with different rhythms. Before taking the discussion any further, however, an important caveat needs to be entered. Historians are seldom able to command a large or tidily structured sample. The evidence that survives, that which can be found, is often patchy, uneven, occasionally fragmentary. The process of gathering it can best be described as serendipity—hence the cautious use of 'some' in the second sentence of this paragraph. The discussion which follows is in no way intended to imply that even a majority of women teachers or women clerks embarked on such journeys; it simply shows what proved possible for a few.

I. Women maintained school teachers

The encounter of women maintained school teachers with formal, state provided and sponsored schooling was sustained and prolonged. Having done well at elementary school they were likely then to become pupil-teachers there—apprentices—and if fortunate and the resources could be found, to go on to formal training at what was then called a Normal School, achieving certification at the end. Without the Normal School, it might nevertheless be possible to achieve certification on the basis of the apprenticeship, reports from Her Majesty's Inspectors of Schools (HMI) and examinations. This was the pattern from the 1840s through to the end of the century, beginning to change only after 1904, when the Board of Education began to dismantle the pupil-teacher system and to funnel all intending teachers into the new maintained secondary schools before proceeding to training (Robinson, 2003; Tropp, 1957).

The early lives of women maintained school teachers thus appeared dominated by formal provision and, on the face of it, difficult to fit into any discussion of movement between formal and informal educational provision. However women could react to this formal provision in a variety of ways. The actual workload was hard and gruelling, dealing not only with inspection and examinations but also the daily grind of unruly classes of fluctuating and often large sizes. Ruth Slate, born in London in 1884 and whom we shall meet again, was deemed 'not strong enough for teaching' (Thompson, 1987, p. 22).[1] Gertrude Tuckwell, an exception to the usual pattern as a young middle-class woman, embarked on elementary school teaching in London in the early 1880s and stuck it out for six years, then in exhaustion succumbing to a bad attack of scarlet fever. On recovery she turned to the less arduous work of organising women's labour unions (Copelman, 1996, pp. 11–14). Marriage bars were not universal before 1914, but few concessions were made to married women with families. Between the 1870s and 1890s the expectation was that they would take no more than four weeks' maternity leave and for that time find and pay a substitute (Copelman, 1996, p. 185). The novelist Richard Church reported the experience of his mother, Lavinia, following his own birth:

> within a few weeks Mother went back to her teaching in an elementary school in the Horseferry Road, Westminster. How she travelled to and fro in that time, I have no idea; but the fatigue of this journey four times a day (for she had to come home to feed me), plus the task of handling some sixty slum urchins from the wilderness of Pimlico, must have tasked her vitality.

Between feeds Richard was cared for by Harriet, the eldest daughter of a large working-class family nearby (Church, 1955, p. 41).

There was not therefore much margin, physically, psychologically or indeed financially, beyond the formal demands made on women elementary school teachers, particularly on women with families. Lavinia Church controlled the family finances with a rod of iron: books and music were to be borrowed from the library. She was disconcerted therefore when the 16-year-old Richard spent one and sixpence out of his first wages on Palgrave's *Golden Treasury* of verse (Church, 1955, pp. 89–90, 94–97). It is not unreasonable to suppose that many women, having achieved the security of a respectable, pensionable job, put their remaining energies into home and family—and survival. Indeed it has been argued that the whole bundle of experience, apprenticeship, inspection, examination, training, if it could be secured, was a deadening one, choking off any intellectual ambition young women —and young men—may have had. Thomas Hardy knew something of the woman teacher's experience for his own sister had been a pupil-teacher and their parents had scrimped and saved to support her subsequently at the Normal School in Salisbury (Tomalin, 2006, pp. 57–60). He used this experience in his novel, *Jude the Obscure*, eventually published in book form in 1895, as the basis for his portrait of the Normal School at 'Melchester' as 'a species of nunnery'. In her early days there his well-read leading female character Sue Bridehead had 'altogether the air of a woman clipped and pruned by severe discipline' (Hardy, 1964 [1895], pp. 139, 146).

Another vivid guide to tensions and disjunctions between the life of the mind glimpsed in reading and training and the grind of the training itself and then classroom work is to be found in the bitter little stories written by James Runciman, teacher turned journalist, collected together as *Schools and Scholars* in 1887. One of his targets was Matthew Arnold, who earned his living as Her Majesty's Inspector of schools, but 'never thought of bestowing a little sweetness and light on the young teachers whose interests he was paid to further' (Runciman, 1887, p. 164). The tensions were lived out too in Runciman's own life and work and seem to have contributed to his early death (see Runciman, Allen, & Stead, 1893).

Yet there were others, men and women, who were able to respond in a more straightforward and positive way to the experience. F. H. Spencer became a pupil-teacher in 1886, then won a scholarship to Borough Road, the British and Foreign School Society Normal School. His father, he noted,

> was one of the type of skilled artisan not by any means uncommon, men of intelligence with intellectual interests which they are only partly able to exercise. 'Going to college' appealed to him and he hardly discriminated between Balliol or Trinity and a Training College for Teachers then in the back streets of South London. (Spencer, 1938, pp. 74–75)

Emerging from Borough Road as a well-qualified and capable teacher, the young Spencer wanted to pursue reading he had first begun there. He discovered the University Extension movement and through its classes began to work for an external London degree. In the course of this he encountered some key figures in the early socialist movement and left teaching for a time to work as a paid researcher for the Fabians. Returning to teaching as head of the Day Department at City of London College he would become one of His Majesty's Inspectors before moving to lead and energise the London County Council's own education inspectorate.

The external degree route was one taken also by women. Wendy Robinson has managed to gather enough evidence to create a database of staff at pupil-teacher centres, the centres created by a number of local authorities to deliver the further study required by pupil-teacher training to complement time in the classroom. Her database comprises 80 women and 73 men; and 68% of the women and 73% of the men either already had or were in the process of completing degrees (Robinson, 2003, pp. 77–78, 82–85). Scholarships, training courses, evening classes and external degree courses were among the means by which the children of late Victorian and Edwardian artisans and white-collar workers could seek intellectual enrichment as well as advancement.

Other women chose to enlarge their reading outside the framework of formal courses and/or become politically active; and union involvement and political activism could develop and hone strength and self-confidence further. When the legal secretary Eva Slawson joined the ILP in 1908, her comments about a woman 'fellow comrade' are illuminating: 'Mrs Shimmins, however, has been a teacher and has passed through college. I am not sure yet whether I like her. She is young and very bright—talks with ease (which I do not) and has a decided manner' (letter of 13 July 1908, Women's Library [WL], 7RSJ/B/01/07; Thompson, 1987, p. 124). Eva was at first tentative; Mrs Shimmins launched straight in. As Etta Dan and Mary Hatch, respondents in the Essex University oral history project on Family

Life and Work Experience before 1918, commented, you built up a certain strength and confidence in encounters and discussions if you had survived four years as a pupil-teacher, two years at a training college and a plethora of demonstration lessons with the Head, the college's Mistress of Method, HMI and fellow-students as audience besides the children you were actually teaching (Dan, 1970–1973, British Library Sound Archives [BLSA], C707/21; Hatch, 1970–1973, BLSA, C707/143).

Between 1900 and 1920 female membership of the National Union of Teachers, the elementary school teachers' union, grew faster than male membership; by 1914, 75% of certificated women teachers were members. Equal pay was already a live issue and from 1904 members of the NUT could join an Equal Pay League; in 1920 a group of women teachers would break away over this issue to form the National Union of Women Teachers (Oram, 1996, p. 3). Formal training, union and political activism all contributed to a developing sense of professional identity and ambition among women teachers which from 1900 converged with suffrage feminism (Copelman, 1996, pp. 202–205, 212–219; Oram, 1996, p. 104). There are fascinating analogies here with the contribution by his union, the Postal Workers, to the education, political and otherwise, of the future Labour cabinet minister, Alan Johnson, in the late twentieth century (Johnson, 2014, esp. pp. 169–174).

Johnson, however, is male. His experiences have a well-defined context and ancestry in the work of trade unions and unionists from the early nineteenth century onwards, to support and educate their members, symbolised by the foundation of Ruskin College at Oxford in 1899 and the creation of the Workers' Educational Association in 1903. The middle-class enthusiasts developing University Extension Lectures were in part responding to this. Yet so often the principal actors and beneficiaries in this history were male. A typical late-nineteenth century audience for Extension Lectures was likely to consist of trade-unionist men and middle-class women (Goldman, 1995). In exploring the world of working-class writers in Britain between the wars, Christopher Hilliard comments sadly on the paucity of women. He shares Claire Langhammer's conclusion that when they married, working women often subordinated their own aspirations to the needs of other family members, especially their children (Hilliard, 2006, pp. 101, 113). We have already seen it: it was what Lavinia Church, the mother of the novelist, had done. It was what Mary Hatch, one of the respondents to the Essex Oral History project, did, single-handedly bringing up three of her own children and two step-sons. It may well be that the fruits of many women's intellectual and emotional explorations are to be found in the lives of their families and the support they gave to their children. This however makes the few direct glimpses we have of such explorations and aspirations the more important.

Less conspicuous for their political activism but developing rich intellectual, cultural and emotional lives outside their work were the young women teachers among whom D. H. Lawrence moved in Nottingham and then in Croydon. It would be foolish to generalise from any aspect of Lawrence's own career about the life of a maintained school teacher; but his early women friends, all teachers—Jessie Chambers, Louie Burrows, Agnes Mason and Helen Corke—although perhaps out of the ordinary, were less extraordinary than Lawrence himself. Their relationships with Lawrence and his ruthless use in his fiction of material from their lives, melded with material from his own, means that we know a great deal more about their experience than might otherwise be the case. It is material to be used with great caution, but it would be foolish to ignore altogether what it suggests about what *might* be made of the woman teacher's life.[2]

All four women had begun as pupil-teachers; of them only Louie Burrows had gone on to college. The others eventually secured certification as teachers by examination. In Helen Corke's case there had simply been no money to go down this route (Corke, 1975, p. 132). Lawrence himself had pursued it, securing an external London degree as a Nottingham University College student, sharing classes there with Louie Burrows. Yet he urged Jessie Chambers' farming family not to support her in doing the same, commenting, 'They grind them all through the same mill'. He may also have had an ulterior motive; he told Jessie herself, 'You might so easily become a blue-stocking, you know' (Chambers, 1935, pp. 81, 82–83).

All the women had had, however, some experience of the teaching at a pupil-teachers' centre and Jessie Chambers remarked that although what was on offer was 'a beggarly makeshift, for me it was wealth beyond price' (Chambers, 1935, p. 45). With friends and colleagues they supplemented their formal work with voracious and eclectic reading. Helen Corke's reading at this stage in her life included Carlyle and evolutionary theory, but also lightweight fiction, Wilkie Collins, Hall Caine, Sarah Grand and Mrs Henry Wood (Corke, 1975, p. 115). Jessie Chambers, urged on by Lawrence, was early on much more ambitious. She and Lawrence read French together, Shakespeare and the poetry of Blake; he encouraged her to attend Saturday morning lectures in Nottingham on the Metaphysical Poets (Chambers, 1935, pp. 56–63; cf. also ch. iv, pp. 94–123). They sought out like-minded friends and in 1909 Lawrence read his essay *Art and the Individual* 'to a little gathering of the Eastwood intelligentsia at the house of a friend' (Chambers, 1935, p. 120). In correspondence with Emile Delavenay in 1933–1935 Jessie Chambers noted that her 'copy of Schopenhauer is in the Scott Library edition ... with the marginal notes that Lawrence made at the time he read the essay on the "Metaphysics of Love"'; and recorded that her present to Lawrence on his twenty-second birthday was a copy of J. L. Motley's *Rise of the Dutch Republic* (letters of 1 November 1933 and 1 February 1935: Chambers (1979)).

Meanwhile Helen Corke had discovered Wagner and Nietzsche; and in the autumn of 1908 she also met Lawrence, newly arrived to teach in the Croydon elementary school where her friend Agnes Mason was his colleague. Corke and Lawrence began to read together in both English and German and while she introduced him to Olive Schreiner's *Story of an African Farm*, he introduced her to the fiction of H. G. Wells, Arnold Bennett and E. M. Forster and to the poetry of Walter de la Mare (Corke, 1975, pp. 157, 160, 184). With literary exploration went exploration of personal and sexual relationships and a kind of moral self-education. Helen Corke had been very close to Agnes Mason and the relationship may well have included some physical intimacy. Later, reading Edward Carpenter's *Love's*

Coming of Age, she would conclude that she was probably bi-sexual (Corke, 1965, p. 13; 1975, pp. 155–156, 162–170, 173–174, 191, 210–211).

The experiences of these young women can be read to show that despite an often brutal daily grind, some young women teachers in maintained schools could find the ambition, appetite and stamina to explore a larger cultural and intellectual world and to experiment with relationships. Their formal training and occupation provided a framework, confidence and opportunities to read and range more widely in their thinking, opportunities which a number of them took. Their sustained encounters with formal educational processes were important in themselves but they were not all-sufficient; these encounters served also to launch the women on a variety of educational journeys of their own making.

II. Women clerks

The surviving papers of two young women clerks, Ruth Slate and Eva Slawson, born in the London area respectively in 1884 and 1882, illuminate the experiences of women who had a much less substantial and extensive experience of formal state schooling to launch them on their educational journeys. Ruth was, as we have seen, deemed 'not strong enough' for teaching; but the reading and writing skills she acquired in elementary school were sufficient to gain her initially a job in a warehouse. From there she moved to a low grade clerical job, while going to night school to learn drawing, composition, arithmetic, book-keeping and mensuration. Although she had to give up the evening classes before completing the course, they had provided enough to enable her to secure a more responsible clerical job in the grocery firm, Kearley & Tonge, in which she stayed for 12 years (Thompson, 1987, pp. 25–39; cf. also pp. 102–103, 111, 132). Ruth's friend Eva began work unhappily in domestic service; but her grandparents who brought her up, scrimped and saved to find the money for shorthand and typing classes, enabling her, thus equipped, to find a job as a secretary in a solicitor's office. She carried on with evening classes, now in grammar and literature, and began to learn French (Slawson, letter of 24 January 1905, WL, 7RSJ/B/01/04; Thompson, 1987, pp. 43, 61, 124).

The drive to secure a cleaner, better paid and altogether higher status job may account for much of this effort; but Eva's classes in literature and French hint at wider intellectual ambitions which, as we shall see, Ruth shared. The ubiquity and variety of evening classes, which gave them opportunities to develop and add to their skills, are important points to stress. These came in two principal forms, from local authorities and from private enterprise; and from the end of the 1880s on there was a positive explosion in both. From 1889 the windfall of the 'whisky money', the proceeds of a duty on spirits, was diverted to the new county and county borough councils, to be spent in the encouragement of technical education. This was very broadly interpreted, embracing everything from French and history through book-keeping and typing to mechanical engineering. From 1893 as well a new Code of government grants for night schools was promulgated, untying them at last from the elementary curriculum. The London County Council was to the fore in seizing both these opportunities, a national pace-maker in this respect as in others; and it gave benign support to the growth of the polytechnics. These had begun in the nineteenth century as voluntary institutions, initially predominantly for youths and adults to learn technical trades complementary to work; but their voluntary nature made it easy to add other subjects, if local demand existed. By 1910–1911 attendance at polytechnic evening classes in London numbered 128,464 people and three of the six most popular subjects were book-keeping, shorthand and French (Heller, 2011, p. 166; cf. also Pennybacker, 1995, p. 43). The polytechnic leader, Regent Street, had by 1910 developed two commercial departments; and between 1905 and 1913 almost 29% of the female students attending classes were estimated as being in white-collar occupations, not far off the 34% of men students in such jobs (Heller, 2011, p. 165).

The private enterprise leader and runaway success story in London was Pitman's. Their pitch to young women was clear and unambiguous, as their 1893 prospectus put it,

> girls would do much better by learning Shorthand and Typewriting (by which, when proficient, they could earn a competency), than in acquiring mechanical dexterity on the piano, which only pays those who have great musical taste and ability, or in endeavouring to earn a living as governesses without having been specially trained in the work. (Quoted in Davy, 1986, p. 125)

By 1904 Pitman's principal 'Metropolitan School' in Southampton Row had between 1500 and 1600 students, a mixture of part-time and full-time. The Pitman motto was 'Learning and Earning' and they endeavoured to spread the burden of their not inconsiderable fees by an instalment system. Like the Regent Street Polytechnic, Pitman's ran a Situations Bureau or employment agency to place their successful students (Heller, 2011, pp. 167–172).

We simply do not know which or whose classes Ruth and Eva attended; the absence of mention of labels may mean that they favoured and/or found more convenient small, private enterprises. In September 1914 Eva was exploring the elocution classes at the City of London College, but quickly pulled out, describing it as a great commercial venture with 'no individual attention' and much 'cram'; she decided to look for private lessons instead (Slawson, letters of 15 September and 9 October 1914, WL, 7RSJ/B/1/13). Her approach provides ample demonstration of the ways in which these young women actively sought out opportunities and discriminated between what was available. They were far from passive recipients of institutional instruction.

At least as important as evening classes to the two young women clerks were two other institutions: the public library and the chapel. By the Public Libraries Act of 1850 local authorities were empowered to provide these out of the rates, if they chose. Initial take-up was slow; but by the last decades of the century they were widespread and heavily used. As we have already seen, Lavinia Church made her family use the library (Church, 1955, pp. 89–90, 94–97). In Manchester at the turn of the century the young telephonist Stella Davies remembered that her father had enrolled every one of his 14 children as soon as they could read (Davies, 1963, p. 62). References to current library books are scattered throughout the correspondence between Eva and Ruth, even when gradually they begin to buy or are given as presents tried and tested favourites. Both read widely and with a fine eclecticism. Among nineteenth-century novelists George Eliot was a particular favourite, to whom they returned time and again. Ruskin's *Sesame and Lilies* was an important discovery. They also ranged extensively among more recent novels, from novels about the position of women, such as Olive Schreiner's *Story of an African Farm*, through Grant Allen's *The Woman Who Did* and Sarah Grand's *The Beth Book* to Hardy and Wells. Nor were they above sampling Marie Corelli; and in the autumn of 1914, when war news was consistently grim, Eva admitted to finding diversion and distraction in the romances of Baroness Orczy.[3]

Their choice of reading also illustrates their developing critical senses and discrimination. In 1904, having been lent Marie Corelli's *God's Good Man*, Ruth expressed her doubts to Eva, 'as a rule there is a very disturbing unhealthy exciting element in her books' (Slate, letter of 20 October 1904, WL, 7RSJ/G/02/02). In May 1908 Ruth recorded in her diary, 'Read *The Story of an African Farm* in lunch hour. Am I presumptuous in feeling that *much* of what I have been thinking and feeling so strongly is here expressed' (Slate, diary entry of 28 May 1908, WL, 7RSJ/A/01/14, f. 31, her emphasis; Thompson, 1987, p. 117). Embarked on H. G. Wells' *The New Machiavelli* in 1913, Eva commented, 'a brilliant but shallow book. Wells remind me of sherbert (sic) which when shot into water causes it to effervesce—he is stimulating, but, I think, transitory' (Slawson, diary entry of 28 June 1913, WL, 7RSJ/G/01/02, f. 15; Thompson, 1987, p. 175). In August 1915, when her half-sister Gertie, a militant suffragette, was expressing a wish to read Hardy's *Jude the Obscure*, she noted that such was the novel's power that it might do good or ill—'Hardy is like a great organ, but he plays in the minor key' (Slawson, diary entry of 4 August 1915, WL, 7RSJ/G/01/12). Their reading and the correspondence they exchanged about it, recall the self-education and intellectual exchanges of the teachers in the Lawrence circle but also carry echoes of the comments and notes on reading that characterise the letters of the women in the Austen circle in the 1810s and of middle-class women throughout the nineteenth century, underlining the importance of correspondence and shared reading outside any institutional framework.

Complementing and enhancing this range was the associational life surrounding chapel. They had first met at the Methodist Chapel in Manor Park, East London in 1903; and chapel structures and friends were sources both of additional suggestions for reading and other sorts of training. It seems plausible to suggest that one of the impulses towards keeping a diary was the Protestant emphasis on the need for a regular moral accounting. Keeping a diary also provided important and regular practice in writing, describing and summarising. It is easier to see this at work for Ruth, since the diaries that have survived run from 1897, when she was 13, to 1909; then, after a break, resume in 1914 (Slate, 1897–1909, 1914–1916, diaries,

WL, 7RSJ/A/01/01–/17). What began as a childish record gained gradually in fluency, sophistication and power; and these gains are reflected also in her correspondence (Slate, 1903–1916, letters to E. Slawson, WL, 7RSJ/G/02/01–/15). Eva's diaries have survived only for the years 1913–1916 (Slawson, 1913–1916, diaries, WL, 7RSJ/G/01/01–/15); but a comparison of these with her letters to Ruth from 1903 to 1916 suggests a similar development (Slawson, 1903–1916, letters to R. Slate, WL, 7RSJ/B/01/01–/14). Summaries of lengthy sermons and addresses also demanded concentration, the recapitulation of arguments and practice in the art of précis. In addition chapel organisations provided practice in public speaking. Both young women taught Sunday school classes and led week-night discussion groups. The experiences were similar to those of Stella Davies in Manchester, where the social life connected with her local Methodist chapel 'made up a great part of our life'. The Mutual Improvement Society met every Monday and there were also regular 'Useful Knowledge' lectures (Davies, 1963, p. 76). Regular chapel-going, traditions of self-examination and moral accounting, of religious instruction and discussion all played their part in the intellectual and moral training and development of these young women.

Like Stella, however, Ruth and Eva, came to find the patriarchal framework of Methodism constraining and began to explore other ways of living an ethical life. Stella's loss of faith and discovery of socialism proceeded together and the cluster of activities around one of Robert Blatchford's Clarion Cycling Clubs replaced chapel as her intellectual and social focus (Davies, 1963, pp. 82–83). For Ruth, the opportunities for such exploration were easier of access than they proved to be for Eva; working in the City, she could and did use her lunch hours to sermon-taste and attend all sorts of lectures and meetings. Her family moved house to different areas of suburban London, with different chapels, several times. Then at the end of 1909 she moved out of the family home and into lodgings in central London. Among the contacts brought by this mobility were Quaker groups. Eva made only one move, from Manor Park to Walthamstow; and became increasingly involved in the work of the Congregational Chapel there, with its charismatic and radical minister Mr James, becoming Superintendent of its Girls' League and Women's Conference.

In counterpoint to this exploration of other Christian denominations' offerings, from 1906–1907 onwards Ruth and Eva became involved not only with more heterodox organisations but also with overtly political ones, more like the Clarion Clubs. Ruth joined the Progressive Thought League, promoting the Congregationalist R. J. Campbell's 'New Theology', and both she and Eva taught at the Hoxton Adult School, which combined religious and social teaching. In the autumn of 1912 Ruth joined the radical feminist group, The Freewoman Discussion Circle. In 1908 Eva joined the Independent Labour Party and the Women's Labour League, retaining her links with the latter when, for reasons which are not clear, she left the ILP in 1912. Both too joined the Women's Freedom League, which broke away from the Pankhursts' Women's Social and Political Union in 1908, being both less militant and more democratic in its structure. While active in the suffrage movement, neither was disposed towards militant or direct action; and on the outbreak of war both emerged as committed pacifists, joining the Fellowship of Reconciliation and later the No Conscription Fellowship.[4] As the sheer range of these involvements indicates, Ruth and Eva had begun to scrutinise and to question everything, from religious faith and practices, through social purpose and the search for the just society, to human relationships and sexuality, including their own. Fairly launched on their courses of self-education, nothing was off-limits.

Ruth's first serious heterosexual relationship had been with a childhood friend, Ewart Johnson, but he died from tuberculosis in the summer of 1903. Subsequently she became engaged to Walter Randall—'Wal'—but he emerged as a tricky, devious young man, and a firm opponent of women's suffrage. The relationship painfully unravelled during the autumn of 1908 and the first months of 1909. In the autumn of 1912 through the Freewoman Circle Ruth met Françoise Lafitte, whom she considered 'a second Olive Schreiner' and they went on to share a flat together, where Ruth sustained Françoise through the birth of her baby, the product of a short-lived 'free union'. Françoise continued her life in free-thinking and radical circles, eventually becoming the partner of Havelock Ellis following the death of his wife Edith (Delisle, 1946).

Although Ruth remained supportive of Françoise and her subsequent relationships, she showed no disposition to follow her example. In the course of 1913 her Quaker connections brought her two new and important male friends, the somewhat older American, David Thomson, and the Englishman, Hugh Jones. David Thomson tried a number of times to persuade Ruth to become his wife and move to the United States with him but she always hesitated. Her feelings for Hugh were somewhat more complex. Initially he considered himself in search of a high ideal of friendship rather than love for a particular individual; and Ruth wrote to Eva in June 1913, 'through me he loves and interprets Woman. He loves Womanhood in me but he does not love *me*. Oh my dear, will that gift ever be mine?' (Slate, letter of 3 June 1913, WL, 7RSJ/G/02/11, her emphasis). Subsequently Hugh was shaken to discover the depths of his personal feelings for Ruth; still hankering after his ideal, he then had bouts of wanting to break off the friendship. Eventually in 1917 they would marry.

Eva had no comparably close male friendships, although there are signs that her office colleague, Frost, would have liked more than a working relationship with her; and she was undoubtedly attracted by Mr James, the Walthamstow Congregationalist minister. Her closest relationship with a contemporary outside her family, apart from her friendship with Ruth, was with the married Minna Simmons, whom she met in the Walthamstow congregation. Minna's husband Will died of tuberculosis early in 1914, while she was still carrying their fourth child. Subsequently Eva and Minna became very close, both emotionally and physically. Eva often spent the night at Minna's house and was present at the birth of the baby, Joan. Eva was familiar with the writing of Edward Carpenter and his celebration of same-sex love and relationships in *Love's Coming of Age* (1896); but she seems never to have acknowledged that his teaching might be applied to her relationship with Minna. In other respects, however, their discussions ranged widely. Having been married, Minna was sceptical about the durability of romance, thinking that 'often the less romantic marriages, built upon kindly, friendly feeling and trust, were the happiest'. Eva, however, felt that, 'one lowers one's standards unless one can feel in some degree a three-fold attraction—physical, mental, spiritual. I do not think I could marry unless I felt this!'. Later on, discussing polygamous relationships, she wrote

> Minna felt she could share a man with me—neither of us felt we could share a man with Lily or Ruth—I think because we recognise they are essentially lovers, and I suppose would in some way possess a decided advantage over us! (Slawson, diary entry of 13 September 1914, WL, 7RSJ/G/01/08, ff.68–69; Thompson, 1987, p. 247—Lily had come to look after Minna's children while Minna trained as a nurse)

Exploring human relationships and their variety was as much a part of their self-education as studying literature, or debating political questions.

Although David Thomson eventually recognised that Ruth would not become his wife, he was still determined to help her and encourage her development. With his financial help and a scholarship, Ruth was able in 1914 to go to Woodbrooke, the Quaker college near Birmingham, where she flourished and secured a formal social science qualification, going on with this to work as a personnel officer for Rowntree's in York. Urged on and helped with the practicalities by Ruth, Eva followed her to Woodbrooke in the autumn of 1915, also on a scholarship. Woodbrooke thus represented a second encounter with a full-time formal educational structure for both women, albeit one not provided by the state.

However the experience of Woodbrooke also tested the limits of the educational experiences both had thus far so energetically pursued. Eva found it hard to establish a structured work pattern. And just as she had initially been intimidated by the self-assurance of 'Comrade Mrs Shimmins' when she first joined the ILP, she and Ruth were also intimidated at first by the self-assurance of other students who had had more formal education before their studies at Woodbrooke. Ruth reflected, 'There is such an abundancy of spirits ... in those who were at school until their twenties and then began on a "profession" which tells me plainly that in our cases a reservoir has been sapped' (Slate, letter of 7 February 1916, WL, 7RSJ/G/02/14; Thompson, 1987, pp. 291–293). Replying, Eva agreed that the college girls had more stamina for examinations, but 'I do think though we have the advantage in a much more intimate knowledge of the suffering side to life—of those who toil— and, I think, perhaps, a deeper appreciation of friendship' (Slawson, letter of 10 February 1916, WL, 7RSJ/B/01/14; Thompson, 1987, pp. 291–293).

In the spring of 1916 Eva was at last beginning to get the measure of a more structured work pattern, when tragically she collapsed and died from undetected diabetes. After Eva's death, Ruth came close to irritation at the stress everyone laid on Eva's humility: 'Much of that humility was the lack of self-confidence both Eva and I have felt to be the curse of our lives & which has been unduly and unhealthily fostered in us by mistaken religious training & hard circumstances' (Slate, diary entry of 24 March 1916, WL, 7RSJ/A/01/17, f. 15; Thompson, 1987, p. 300). The contrast with the confidence of the 'college girls' is marked. Yet both women had undergone and slowly begun to comprehend a complex mix of experiences which made up an educational process stretching well into adulthood.

Interestingly the range of Ruth Slate's and Eva Slawson's reading and their consequent thorough questioning of human relationships were not so very different from those of the young women teachers in D. H Lawrence's circle in the years up to 1912. Yet this range and this questioning were the products of what were, on the face of it, very different educational experiences. Ruth's and Eva's encounters with formal schooling were much more limited and widely separated in time—elementary school and then Woodbrooke; between these there were only the part-time and occasional encounters of evening classes. How do we classify such encounters—is semi-formal an adequate description? And much more important, how do we classify and characterise the experience in listening, concentrating, re-capitulating an argument, summarising, writing and speaking provided by involvement in the activities of the chapel and subsequently by the other organisations, discussion groups and political associations, which Ruth and Eva joined? Determination was undoubtedly required to persist, to seek out reading, discussion, organisational structures which would stretch the mind and tax the stamina; was it qualitatively different from the determination which drove young women pupil-teachers on through the grind of training and then classroom life, without entirely losing sight of intellectual preoccupations and ideas?

A simple distinction between formal and informal modes of education is too limited to capture the richness and complexity of these young women's interactions with all the institutional structures of their society, whether labelled 'school', 'college', chapel, club, public library—or family and friends. The interplay is continuous and infinitely complex and one in which their own agency steadily grew in importance. Nor was this process limited to the years of childhood and/or adolescence. It was not time-stopped in any way; it was a project for living a life as fully as possible, always learning.

Disclosure statement

No potential conflict of interest was reported by the author.

Notes

1. The primary sources which lie both behind my discussion of Ruth Slate and her great friend, Eva Slawson, and that of Thompson (1987) have been deposited in The Women's Library [WL] now in the custody of the London School of Economics, in the collection 7RSJ. Where possible, references are made to both manuscript and book. In no sense is this meant to imply criticism of Ms Thompson's work. She is owed a great debt of gratitude for rescuing the papers and making them available to a wider audience; and her commentary, dating and transcriptions (failing only to indicate editorial omissions) are models of scrupulous accuracy. The material is so rich, however, that other and different questions can also be asked of it; and my efforts should be seen as complementary to hers.

2. Lawrence sustains a whole academic industry. Relevant to this discussion are: Boulton (1979), Chambers (1935, 1979), Corke (1965, 1975), Delavenay (1979), Lawrence (1989 [1915]) and Worthen (1991).
3. Examples include mentions of *The Beth Book* in Slawson (letter of 19 September 1913, WL, 7RSJ/B/01/12); *Sesame and Lilies* in Slawson (letter of 23 August 1904, WL, 7RSJ/B/01/10); *The Woman Who Did* in Slawson (diary entry of 16 August 1913, WL, 7RSJ/G/01/03, ff. 2–3; Thompson, 1987, p. 180); Wells' *Ann Veronica* in Slawson (diary entry of 16 December 1913, WL, 7RSJ/G/01/04, f. 1); Baroness Orczy in Slawson (diary entry of 19 September 1914, WL, 7RSJ/G/01/08, f. 86) and Slawson (diary entries of 24 and 27 September 1914, WL, 7RSJ/G/01/09, ff. 10 and 22); and *Life of George Eliot, Sesame and Lilies* and *Romola* in Slate (letters of 3 March, 10 April and 30 May 1904, WL, 7RSJ/G/02/02).
4. The account of Ruth's and Eva's lives in the preceding and following paragraphs is drawn from the correspondence and diaries already cited and from the editor's introduction and framing summaries for each chapter in Thompson (1987). For further reading on the organisations named and their context, see Delap (2007) and Rowbotham (2010).

References

Boulton, J. T. (Ed.). (1979). *The letters of D. H. Lawrence. Vol. 1: September 1901–May 1913*. Cambridge: Cambridge University Press.
British Library Sound Archives (BLSA). C707/21 and C707/143, interviews given by Etta Dan and Mary Hatch to the Essex University Oral History Project, 'Family Life and Work Experience before 1918', 1970–1973.
Chambers, J. (1935). *D. H. Lawrence: A personal record*. London: Cape.
Chambers, J. (1979). The collected letters of Jessie Chambers. *D. H. Lawrence Review*, 12(1–2) (G. J. Zytaruk, Ed.).
Church, R. (1955). *Over the Bridge. An Essay in Autobiography*. London: Heinemann.
Copelman, D. M. (1996). *London's women teachers: Gender, class and feminism 1870–1930*. London: Routledge.
Corke, H. (1965). *D.H. Lawrence: The Croydon years*. Austin: University of Texas Press.
Corke, H. (1975). *In our infancy: An autobiography*. Cambridge: Cambridge University Press.
Davies, C. S. (1963). *North Country bred, a working-class family chronicle*. London: Routledge & K. Paul.

Davy, T. (1986). 'A cissy job for men; a nice job for girls': Women shorthand typists in London 1900–39. In L. Davidoff & B. Westover (Eds.), *Our work, our lives, our words: Women's history and women's work* (pp. 124–144). Basingstoke: Macmillan Education.

Delap, L. (2007). *The feminist avant-garde. Transatlantic encounters of the early twentieth century.* Cambridge: Cambridge University Press.

Delavenay, E. (1979). D.H. Lawrence and Jessie Chambers: The traumatic experiment. *D.H. Lawrence Review, 12,* 305–325.

Delisle, F. R. (1946). *Friendship's odyssey.* London: Heinemann (Françoise Lafitte's autobiography, writing as Françoise Roussel Delisle).

Durkheim, E. (1956 [1922]). *Education and sociology* (S. D. Fox, Trans.). Glencoe, IL: Free Press.

Goldman, L. (1995). *Dons and workers: Oxford and adult education since 1850.* Oxford: Clarendon Press.

Hardy, T. (1964 [1895]). *Jude the obscure.* London: Macmillan.

Heller, M. (2011). *London clerical workers, 1880–1914.* London: Pickering & Chatto.

Hilliard, C. (2006). *To exercise our talents. The democratization of writing in Britain.* Cambridge, MA: Harvard University Press.

Johnson, A. (2014). *Please, Mister Postman: A memoir.* London: Bantam Press.

Lawrence, D. H. (1989 [1915]). *The rainbow* (M. Kinkead-Weekes, Ed.). Cambridge: Cambridge University Press.

Oram, A. (1996). *Women teachers and feminist politics, 1900–1939.* Manchester: Manchester University Press.

Pennybacker, S. D. (1995). *A vision for London 1889–1914: Labour, everyday life and the LCC experiment.* London: Routledge.

Robinson, W. (2003). *Pupil teachers and their professional training in pupil-teacher centres in England and Wales 1870–1914.* Lampeter: Edwin Mellen Press.

Rose, J. (2001). *The intellectual life of the British working classes.* New Haven: Yale University Press.

Rowbotham, S. (2010). *Dreamers of a new day: Women who invented the twentieth century.* London: Verso.

Runciman, J. (1887). *Schools and scholars.* London: Chatto & Windus.

Runciman, J., Allen, G., & Stead, W. T. (1893). *Side lights* (J. F. Runciman, Ed.). London: Fisher Unwin.

Spencer, F. H. (1938). *An inspector's testament.* London: The English Universities Press Ltd.

Sutherland, G. (2015). *In search of the new woman: Middle-class women and work in Britain 1870–1914.* Cambridge: Cambridge University Press.

The Women's Library (WL). At the LSE: the papers of Ruth Jones, nee Slate, boxes 7RSJ/A/01/01–/17, 7RSJ/B/01/01–/14, 7RSJ/G/01/01–/14, 7RSJ/G/02/01–/15.

Thompson, F. (1945 [1939]). *Lark Rise to Candleford.* London: Oxford University Press.

Thompson, T. (Ed.). (1987). *Dear girl: The diaries and letters of two working women (1897–1917).*

Tomalin, C. (2006). *Thomas Hardy: The time-torn man.* London: Viking Penguin.

Tropp, A. (1957). *The school teachers. The growth of the teaching profession in England and Wales from 1800 to the present day.* London: Heinemann.

Worthen, J. (1991). *D.H. Lawrence: The early years 1885–1912.* Cambridge: Cambridge University Press.

Home education: then and now

Richard Davies
Aberystwyth University, UK

Elective Home Education is a legal, minority approach to the compulsory education of children. I review the potential contribution of the historical analysis of 'domestic pedagogies', presented in this Special Issue, for home education practice in the UK. By drawing on narratives of a period at the cusp of the perceived normalcy of 'schooling', I consider an alternative discourse to articulate the purpose of, and approaches to, education. In particular, I focus on the family not only as the site for educational practices, but also as critical for our understanding of what constitutes a 'suitable education'. Along the way, I show how distinctions, common in home education practice, illuminate the historical debates on 'domestic education'. I conclude by suggesting we cannot disassociate discussions of a suitable home education from the family within which such an education occurs.

For most children, education begins, and develops, within the home. Where it does not we consider it a tragedy. In modern industrial societies this usually runs contemporaneously with a period of compulsory *schooling*. An increased period of compulsory, state-funded education is seen as an indicator of national development (for example, by the OECD). Late nineteenth-century England saw a number of acts of parliament which consolidated both state-funded and private schooling (see Gillard, 2011). The result was a largely universal system of elementary education, extended to secondary level in the iconic 1944 Education Act. The period 1750–1900 thus represents a period in which England moved from sporadic opportunities for education outside the home to a situation in which '… it became increasingly difficult to find many who had had no encounter at all with formal provision' (Sutherland, this issue).

In the twenty-first century, the ubiquity of schooling is so pervasive in contemporary society that in many places 'education' has become synonymous with 'schooling', and the role of parents reduced to that specified by home–school contacts (see DfE, 2013). Yet, even a superficial review of home life shows the variety of ways in which children learn from their everyday practices, and how vital these are to living a reasonable life.

At the same time, for a small proportion of children today—about 80,000 in the UK—the home provides a central place for their education (Badman, 2009). Elective Home Education (EHE), legal in the UK, occurs when parents take direct responsibility for all aspects of their children's education. The majority of these children do not attend school, although about 400 'flexi-schoolers' will attend school part-time. It is the education of these *EHE children* which is the focus of this paper, though it is worth noticing at the outset that they differ in many ways from those children who, historically, experienced a 'domestic education'.

As a philosopher and EHE practitioner, my approach is to consider the implications of the papers in this Special Issue for contemporary EHE. This paper comprises both an explicit commentary on, and a substantive argument grounded in, the historical studies in this Special Issue. It develops a deeper understanding of contemporary home education practices alongside a review and critique of the previous papers. This is a two-fold undertaking. The first task is to interrogate the papers through highlighting conceptual distinctions familiar in EHE and informal education discourses; the second is to interrogate present practices in the light of the narratives presented.

I begin by reviewing the landscape of EHE in the UK. I then consider the various historically situated analyses presented in this Special Issue, before developing two key themes for consideration by contemporary EHE practitioners (usually parents) and researchers.

I. Home education: now

The post-war education settlement, enshrined in the 1944 Education Act and reiterated in the 1996 Education Act, requires that:

The parent of every child of compulsory school age shall cause him to receive efficient full-time education suitable—

(a) to his age, ability and aptitude, and
(b) to any special educational needs he may have, either by regular attendance at school or otherwise. (Education Act, 1996, p. 7)

EHE falls under the 'or otherwise' provision of the Acts. A parent is entitled to provide a 'suitable education' without undue interference from the state. What is to count as a 'suitable education' remains unclear (see Davies, 2015). Present case law, reflecting the Convention on the Rights of the Child (UN, 1989, Article 29), holds that a suitable education:

> ... primarily equips a child for life within the community of which he is a member, rather than the way of life in the country as a whole, as long as it does not foreclose the child's options in later years to adopt some other form of life if he wishes to do so. (Woolf, 1985)

Such a wide definition means that children who are 'home educated' or 'flexi-schooled' represent a diverse group with different educational experiences, and that EHE practitioners articulate many different reasons for choosing to home educate (see Morton, 2010). (It is worth noting that, given the difficulty in identifying the EHE population, there are inevitable sampling issues in UK-based empirical studies.) Simply stated, the only element these parents necessarily have in common is that they have decided to home educate their children as opposed to relinquishing that responsibility to the school. Research suggests moreover that EHE practitioners' objectives change over time: EHE practitioners are on a journey in which their understanding of education and the home develops, and becomes more complex (see Thomas, 1998). Their relationship with schooling also becomes more complex, with many home educated children entering formal education as external examinations become significant.

Having pointed to the diversity of EHE practitioners, it is worth noting some broad trends. Some EHE researchers have sought to identify 'autonomous learning' or 'natural learning' as at the heart of authentic EHE practices (see Thomas, 1998). Whilst there may be some evidence for this as a preference among EHE practitioners, this does not preclude the use of formal curricula to structure home education. So, autonomous learning advocates would emphasise the centrality of children's exploration, play and learning in the context of the everyday. According to this approach, children develop their own interests and these are to be 'cultivated' and supported. Other families seek to provide a coherent curriculum either through online programmes, for example, the ACE programme (see www.acemi nistries.com/homeschool), or one individually tailored to their children. For all groups, however, some autonomous learning is important and this tends to be the focus when groups of EHE practitioners and their children meet together.

It is worth noting a distinction between those EHE practitioners who chose to home educate because they see it as a preferable option regardless of the quality of local schools, and those who chose to do so because of some deficit in the local provision (see Morton, 2010). These deficits include such issues as bullying, or failure to respond to special needs. Whilst the first group choose to home educate on grounds of particular conceptions of the family, the latter group are often choosing based on circumstances not of their own making, in particular, the perceived failure of the school to adequately respond to the parents' concerns.

As I noted earlier, EHE is not a coherent movement as such, but defined negatively, in that the children, of compulsory 'school' age, are not full-time school attendees. In being defined, politically, against the school, EHE is often considered in the light of the perceived normalcy of the school and school-based discourses about education. In such discourses the idea of 'natural' play-based learning is seen as an idealised, romantic view of childhood incompatible with the educational needs of citizens in a post-industrial society. Both this view, however, and that of a laissez faire account of autonomous learning can be challenged if we adopt a general view of 'a suitable education' (see Davies, 2015). In that analysis, any particular approach to the education of children can only be justified in so far as it contributes to the child's ability to live a 'good life', rather than by measuring it against an ideal of childhood or the perceived needs of citizens. The critical question is how one specifies the good life, and what abilities, dispositions, knowledge, etc. are necessary to pursue it (see Davies (2003) for a consideration of these latter issues).

As Sutherland (this issue) points out, the period leading up to 1900 represents the last period when children's education was not dominated by a view of education embedded in the discourse of the school. In contemporary policy and public debate, however, the school, and discourses which relate specifically to the school, are taken to be *the* discourse about the education of children. Alternative forms of education which reject such discourses are perceived with suspicion. EHE practitioners today operate in different legal, political and social contexts to parents of the period 1750–1900. Considering a period when school education was less normative may, however, offer new insights for contemporary EHE, just as examining the historical examples through this lens may shed new light on domestic pedagogy in the period before 1900. My approach is, therefore, to seek general themes and resonances between the historical analysis and contemporary EHE practice; I begin with a more general review of the Special Issue as a whole.

II. Domestic pedagogies: then

It is clear from the papers in this Special Issue that the theme of 'domestic pedagogy' is a wide-ranging one. This collection is diverse in terms of the objects of study, methodological approaches and historical period. As a non-historian, EHE practitioner and philosopher of education, I am concerned with the 'resonances' of the historical analysis of the previous papers with contemporary practices of home education. Shortly, I will explore a number of specific connections between *past* and *present*, but first I will broadly review the historical narratives, framing them in terms of 'domestic' and 'pedagogy'. In part I want to set out some of the different interpretations of these key terms which are used within this Special Issue, but also to offer a synthesis of this historical diversity with which to direct my own argument. Following this I draw on the accounts, especially the analysis of Charlotte Mason (de Bellaigue) and the Godwin–Wollstonecraft household (Halsey, Grenby), as well as earlier work (Davies, 2013a, 2015) to develop an account of 'education as upbringing'.

Domestic

In contemporary EHE practice, it is rare to hear reference to 'domestic education', rather the term of 'home' is preferred. Yet there does seem to be more at stake than mere changing usage. As well as underlining the materiality of the house, the *domus*, the term 'domestic' also draws attention to a range of household relationships. In the past, such relationships included those between family members, as well as—in the elite families reflected in many of the papers in this issue— the family's retinue of staff. The 'domestic' revealed in the historical analyses is a structured, semi-public microcosm reflecting the particular character of middle- and upper-class lifestyles of the period. By contrast, the use of 'home' in contemporary home education and homeschooling conjures up a sense of being 'part of', so one feels 'homesick' or 'home is where the heart is', and as such it differs from the materiality of a dwelling place, however permanent. The difference between 'domestic' and 'home' is not simply a matter of changing usage, but reflects shifting models towards a more nuclear family and the kinds of values, including a distrust of a public sphere dominated by the state, that underpin some EHE practitioners' rejection of the school (see for example, Taylor's (1989) account of the shifting conception of the family).

'Domestic' is concerned with both the materiality of house and home, and with a particular institutional arrangement articulated in terms of expected roles and duties. For girls of the eighteenth century especially the household was not only the site of their education, but its purpose. Commenting on Eliza Heywood's 'Alderman Saving', Halsey notes:

> His comments reflect his belief that a woman's proper role is to manage her household … and a dislike of women's increasing involvement in the public sphere. Such sentiments were not unusual. (Halsey, this issue)

Although such an account looks *inward*, as Grenby points out 'Godwin's private household itself functioned as a semi-public schoolroom' (Grenby, this issue) with visitors joining in 'the families educational practices'. In relation to education, in elite families particularly, domestic education looked *outwards*; quoting Carlson, Grenby argues that Godwin saw family '"as a public-oriented relation" and "home as a sphere of enquiry among familiars"' (Grenby, this issue). Such a 'public, pedagogical family' (Grenby, this issue) is reflected in the new children's literature Grenby discusses. Thus, we can mark out a concern with both the 'outward' and the 'inward' approaches to education; distinguishing a *domestic education* from a *domesticating education*. This distinction was often at the heart of debates in the eighteenth century. Halsey (this issue) notes a concern with 'the relative value of a public or private education … and … the proper occupations for women'. There is both an expectation, and emerging critique, that a domestic education is particularly appropriate for girls, whilst boys will in time attend a school. At least part of the difficulty is the perceived inadequacy of public schools in general, for both boys and girls: dangers, moral and intellectual, lurked in the public school.

Thus, in the late eighteenth century, elite families undertook their 'domestic education' at the intersection of the public and the private. The educators were themselves educated and content in the public domain. Many of these women were, as Cohen (this issue) argues, confident pedagogues and able to make available for publication their own teaching resources. At the same time, the fictional, conduct literature and non-fictional accounts continually underlined tensions between the possible dangers (often intellectual dangers) to girls of receiving all their education at home, and the possible, moral and reputational, dangers of attending school. Whilst Moll Flanders' story highlighted the fact that 'even the domestic hearth and home may be rendered unsafe by education' (Halsey, this issue), schooling offered a variety of snares. The moral dangers attributed to schools, whether real or imagined, reflected the perceived safety of the parental gaze, and girls' lack of 'worldliness'—valued in itself—which made them vulnerable to the advances of unscrupulous men and the infectious vanities of their peers. Thus, schools opened girls up to, as Gisbourne warned, the 'pernicious society of those who are not so well principled as themselves' (Halsey, this issue), and the various licentious vices hinted at in Halsey's first illustration (see Halsey, this issue, Figure 1).

These perceived intellectual dangers, the acquisition of various 'surface accomplishments' of dubious worth (see Halsey, this issue), reflected perhaps, the influence of broader social movements. MacIntyre (1985) has discussed more fully the processes by which a society's ethical and political certainties are fragmented and called into question. The first movement he identifies is a decline in a communally agreed discourse about the purpose of human life, and especially a purpose which is tied to one's position within society. In the late eighteenth century, the view that children were being prepared to occupy the social positions of their parents was, at least for elite families, beginning to be disputed. Thus, 'the vigour of the debate surrounding female education was at least partly generated by uncertainty and fears over changing norms and standards of female behaviour' (Halsey, this issue). A girl's purpose in life was no longer simply to marry a suitable man. Rather, educational thinkers, such as Wollstonecraft and Edgeworth (see Grenby, this issue) in their different ways were articulating a more complex account of the development of valuable dispositions, skills and abilities. The second movement identified by MacIntyre (1987) is the rapidly increasing body of knowledge which precludes the possibility of it being known and understood by a single mind. From the late eighteenth century, it was increasingly felt that a well-rounded education needed a number of educators (as in a school) rather than one's parents. Elite families sought to respond in other ways, through the use of private tutors, for example, but even elementary education was deemed to be demanding. The late nineteenth-century 'Mothers Education Course' required students to develop not only a knowledge of how to educate, but also the increasingly complex content of that education (see de Bellaigue, this issue).

Gender also intersected with class. For some young women the rise of schools offered the possibility of pursuing higher status, white-collar jobs. These women, from less well-off households, with due diligence in school and in post-school education, had the opportunity to take up positions as school teachers or clerks. *Public* schooling offered an *alternative* to following their mothers; a means of escaping domesticity, although the work was particularly demanding, especially during early training (see Sutherland, this issue). Interestingly, the less well-documented education of the working class seems to reflect the most static situation, in which children reproduced the social lives of their parents and families. There was little gendered difference in the rates of education at home and at school, and most children received a mixture of both. Boys tended to follow the job profiles of their parents and following school were apprenticed to their fathers, or close male relatives (see Crone, this issue). Girls similarly appeared to follow mothers into domesticity and domestic service. The dilemmas, in terms of school attendance for working-class families, were more related to religious affiliation or availability of schools than to concerns about the appropriateness of school or home education.

It was in elite families then that the dilemma of *schooling* was most pertinent. In such families, an *outwardly facing* domestic education utilised the resources of the home, family and wider community (friends, mutual societies, etc.) to enable children (and young adults) to develop, as Wollstonecraft put it, as 'free, rational and virtuous'. There remained the possibility for education to be shared between parents and suitable teachers in schools, though a number of the papers in this issue reflect the tension in such arrangements (see, for example, Grenby, this issue; Halsey, this issue). In the same period, an *internally facing* domestic education remained less clear about the advantages of a wide educational aspiration, but rather was disposed to protect the child, especially girls, in the home (see Cohen, this issue).

But a *domesticating education* could be as problematic for the educator as much as the child. The implication for the mother is perhaps best illuminated in a letter to the *Parents' Review*. Here, 'Mater' admitted being ground down by the demands of running a home, educating the children and playing the expected wider role in society, all without an entourage of servants (de Bellaigue, this issue). The response of the readers and editors of the *Review* was practical, but it neglected the political aspect; it (simply) required better self and household management from 'Mater' herself. This is a matter which cannot be ignored in relation to contemporary home education, where mothers are usually still the primary educators.

Pedagogy

So far I have been following the terminology of many of the papers in referring to domestic 'education' rather than 'pedagogy'. Drawing now on Hamilton (1999), and with reference to the other papers in this Special Issue, I distinguish between several uses of the term 'pedagogy'.

Historically, 'pedagogy' has been used in relation to three distinct approaches to education: the role of the pedagogue; the analysis of methods of instruction; and an analysis of education as a political practice. According to Hamilton (1999) the dominant use of the term during the eighteenth and nineteenth centuries was to describe the analysis of methods of instruction, which reflected the emergence of mass schooling. However, the *original* pedagogue of the classical era, often a slave, had particular responsibility for the moral development of the child. In order to learn to *be* virtuous one needed, first, to *act* virtuously. The role of the pedagogue was to provide direction as to what virtue demanded of this child, given their status, in a particular situation. The role was not limited to particular times or places, rather the child learnt from the modelling of the pedagogue in everyday situations (see Davies, 2003). This was also a long-term relationship, as the pedagogue would provide support to the child as they prepared for, and continued, their more formal education. MacIntyre (1999) articulates something similar as the primary educative role of all parents and this reflects experiences of many home educators, especially those in the 'autonomous learning' tradition (see Thomas & Pattison, 2007). This approach emphasises a 'being with' your child and that learning *emerges* from responding to, and seeing others respond to, everyday experiences.

The emergence of a perceived need to improve the efficiency of distinctively educational practices saw a separation of the content of educational practices from the methods employed to support children's learning. The latter aspect became the focus of 'pedagogy' as a distinct area of study. As Hamilton (1999) notes, this both challenged the previously held belief that content and method of instruction were necessarily linked, and focussed attention on what teachers *did* rather than what pupils *learnt*. It also led to the possibility of seeing education as a technical or mechanical process turning 'raw materials' (i.e. children) into young adults with the required knowledge, skills and dispositions, using universally available methods. Thus, the preparation of teachers in Sutherland's account (this issue) displays the importance of the correct technique. Charlotte Mason's desire to open a college for women to learn how to be mothers equally emphasises the need for knowledge about how to perform this role. She argued that 'mothers must master a "science of education" and direct the instruction of their children accordingly' (de Bellaigue, this issue). (At the same time, however, as will be discussed below, Mason's use of ideas from, for example, Pestalozzi, tempers this technicist account of education (see Biesta, Allan, and Edwards (2014) for a review of the educational research and the science of education).)

The third use of the term, emerging in the twentieth century, is in relation to 'critical pedagogies' which seeks to reunite content and method, as well as place educational practices explicitly within political and politicised discourses. Critical pedagogies, as Darder, Baltodano, and Torres (2009, p. 2) note:

> ... loosely evolved out of the yearning to give shape and coherence to the theoretical landscape of radical principles, beliefs and practices that contributed to an emancipatory idea of democratic schooling.

As well as concerns with democratic forms of schooling, critical pedagogies have tended to focus on the reproduction of power relations, the truly humanising potential of education, and especially the silencing of marginalised groups with schooling. Darder et al. (2009), whilst locating the emergence of critical pedagogies from the 1930s onwards, nevertheless identify educational theorists, such as Dewey, as offering the foundations for its emergence. Mason's identification with a tradition of education drawing on Pestalozzi and Froebel also places her in one of the foundational traditions of critical pedagogy, and it is also perhaps not too farfetched to see progressive figures, such as Wollstonecraft and Godwin, as in the vanguard of such approaches. Certainly Charlotte Mason's influence on the homeschooling movement, which often situates itself in distinctively critical pedagogical tradition, is indicative (for example, https://simplycharlottemason.com/).

In general terms, it is clear that when discussing 'pedagogy' one needs to be clear about the object under scrutiny. In the case of domestic pedagogies, and home education, particular issues become critical: are we concerned with the activity of the pedagogue, or particular techniques of instruction, and if so, what different approaches to instruction? To what extent do the debates concern, primarily, political and social issues, beyond questions of learning and child development? For example, in recent years, in the UK, discourse about EHE has become increasingly politicised, through a number of reports and consultations, perhaps the most notorious being the Badman Review (Badman, 2009) which argued that there needed to be greater state involvement in EHE (see Lees (2014) for an analysis). The recommendations have not been implemented following a change in government.

III. Towards illumination: a few distinctions

I have argued that the education of children, wherever it occurs and whoever is supporting that education, is legitimate in so far as it contributes to the ability of the child to live life well (see Davies, 2013a, 2013b, 2015). Developing a distinctively Aristotelian account of the flourishing life underpins that argument. Yet it is also possible to articulate a weaker claim to educational legitimacy, on the basis that that life can be lived in better or worse ways, without specifying a substantive general account of what makes a life better or worse. Education should contribute to an increased likelihood of living a better life. Clearly education is not the only element required to support a child; this more general task I identify as 'upbringing'. Education, in its various forms, is part of upbringing and this general account sits well with the present case law on EHE; namely that the child be prepared for life in their community in such a way as not to foreclose their future options.

Such an account also sits well with the analysis of various forms of 'domestic pedagogies' included in this issue. De Bellaigue's analysis of Charlotte Mason's philosophy locates education within upbringing, and there are hints that Godwin, More and Wollstonecraft equally saw education as intrinsically embedded in enabling children to live 'better' lives. Crone indicates how significant the home was for the development of those occupational skills necessary as a member of the working class. In some cases this education took the form of children engaging in 'adult activities', for example Godwin's children's lectures where the children were not to be 'treated as a child' (Grenby, this issue), or as a form of apprenticeship to a parent or close relative, as was the case with working-class children. In some cases this was a more formal introduction to what we might term 'subjects' or 'academic disciplines', as when Godwin's son went to school; in other cases it was a form of educational 'quest' about what was worth doing in life, as in the case of Ruth Slate and Eva Slawson (see Sutherland, this issue). Accordingly, in this section I want to explore two distinctions which are reflected in the papers; namely, the distinction between institutions and practices, and between formal and informal education. In conclusion I want to draw attention to two perennial questions in education: its purpose and what approaches are effective. I show that not only are they interconnected, but that the papers in this Special Issue offer useful resources in addressing these questions for EHE practitioners.

After noting that the 'new children's literature' was closely bound up with home education and that it valorised private education whilst demonising public schooling, Grenby (this issue) notes, however, that: 'the line between home and school education was often very blurred', 'the debate on public versus private education was not always as polarised as we might imagine'; he cites Edgeworth who argued that 'the "solid advantages" of school education must be "secured by previous domestic instruction"'.

Grenby also draws attention to Mary Wollstonecraft's aspiration for 'a middle ground between the inadequate pedagogy and supervision of boarding-schools and the confinement of an adult-dominated "private" education' (Grenby, this issue). Neither option was appealing, both the school and the family were seen to bring educational advantages. He argues that in fact the:

> ... new children's literature served a hybrid private–public educational model than it did domestic education alone. (Grenby, this issue)

At the other end of the social spectrum Crone identifies the contribution of both schools and homes in providing an education for most working-class children.

Sutherland's analysis of the post-school educational exploits of women schoolteachers and clerks identifies the significant role of formal and informal educational establishments played in these biographies. As I noted previously, she comments that 'it became increasingly difficult to find many who had had no encounter at all with formal provision' (Sutherland, this issue). She goes on to say that '... the interesting questions [are] about the relationships between [school] and other educational experiences in individual lives' (Sutherland, this issue). Halsey also explores this territory through the medium of fictional representations of school and education, through which the writers of such 'conduct literature' engage in 'a vigorous and often heartfelt debate about female education' (Halsey, this issue). Attending to Moll Flander's education, she also notes that it could be seen 'as reflecting a broader ambivalence about the benefits of educating women at home' (Halsey, this issue) and the previously mentioned dangers of the hearth (Halsey, this issue). The issue is not simply about the potential of domestic education, but 'the relative value of a public or private education' (Halsey, this issue).

This raises a more basic problem in need of clarification, namely a distinction between *institutions* and *practices*. The school is a distinctively *educational institution*, by which I mean that although it does more than educate, its raison d'être is educational. The *family* is not a distinctively educational institution, but rather defined in part by a commitment to the upbringing of children. One element of upbringing is education, so the family is an institution in which education is a necessary feature, but only periodically central, and more often a 'by-product' of everyday family life. We can read the concerns with both the family and school in two ways. The first is a concern with the educational value of the *practices* in which children are engaging, and the second is with the *institutional* setting of such practices. Some of the debate in the preceding papers tends to collapse this distinction, as perhaps did their subjects.

This distinction helps to clarify the debate by identifying two distinct questions of contemporary significance: what is the purpose of education for children (the practice), and what are the best (institutional) arrangements to support people's learning? Sutherland helpfully develops this latter point in terms of a formal/informal distinction which focuses on not only the institution, but also the kinds of approaches to education which support learning. Sutherland asks:

> There has been a tendency ... to construct a false dichotomy between formal and informal ways of learning, one which has increased in artificiality as the vogue for large schemes of mass schooling has grown in societies. ... It is more helpful to see formal/informal as two poles .... (Sutherland, this issue)

Grenby also notes that '[p]ublic schooling ... was often extremely informal, sourced on an *ad hoc* and intermittent basis ...' (Grenby, this issue). A continuum model, in which educators position themselves between the informal and formal poles, seems more reflective of experiences than a strict dichotomy (see Jeffs & Smith, 1999). In practice, however, there are a number of dimensions which might be characterised as formal–informal. In addition to institutional arrangements, we could consider, for example, curriculum, adult–child relationships, learning spaces and lesson structure (as well as system structure, which is Grenby's point). It is possible to imagine educational practices which are located in different places on the continuum depending on which dimension of that practice we are focussing on. The autonomous learning advocates in home education will emphasise the need for informality in terms of curriculum and have a certain ambivalence on learning spaces as this will depend on the child. Other home educators follow a formal curriculum whilst using informal learning spaces. In both cases we can see similar levels of informal adult–child relationships. Equally, we do see schools following a loosely formal curriculum, using informal spaces, with formal relationships between adults and children (though rarely in the UK).

These histories of 'domestic pedagogies' show the variety of ways education is conducted with complex mixes of formality and informality. They also raise two key questions concerning the purpose and effective approaches for the education of children and, particularly in this paper, for EHE.

IV. Towards illumination: EHE

Purpose

That education ought to increase the likelihood of children living better lives seems uncontentious. The devil, as always, is in the detail. Working-class children in the nineteenth century required, minimally, the wherewithal to earn an income, and in an increasingly literate society a basic level of 'the 3Rs'. For parents of working-class children there was more concern with the availability of resources than the purpose of education (as Crone indicates). For wealthy families in the period 1750–1900 the matter was not settled. Wollstonecraft's call for an education that promoted freedom, rationality and virtue was clear, but lacked the specificity required to inform educational activity. As a statement about the characteristics of a family, however, the ideas of Wollstonecraft (and Godwin) did begin to provide some narrative substantiation of the purpose of education. They expressed their aspirations for the children in terms of the kinds of people they aspired for them to be, and they expressed it in publically acceptable terms.

Educational purpose, in the contemporary discourses of schools, tends to be set out in terms of what children will be able to do, unrelated to their particularities, or often to any perceived future requirements. Often these purposes are set out in the form of universal 'learning outcomes', indicating what the child should know or be able to do. By contrast, for both the working-class and elite families in the past, the purpose of education was set out in terms of practices which were deemed valuable and were articulated *through* family life. It is probably inevitable that there was, and is, disagreement on the purpose of education; what marks out the historical debates as different from the twenty-first century debate is that, in the past, arguments about such purposes were *not* conducted in terms of decontextualised 'learning outcomes'. The particular visionary insight of Wollstonecraft was to articulate purpose in terms which would, within her social circle, gain widespread acceptance. It is not only that visitors to the Godwin–Wollstonecraft household appear to have engaged in educational activities, but that they were inspired by their value.

One of the difficulties for EHE is a perceived expectation that *educational purpose* must either be rejected, or articulated in terms reticent of the style of school 'learning outcomes'. What emerges from the historical accounts is an alternative formulation of education articulated in terms of substantive claims about the kinds of families within which upbringing occurs, and the aspirations parents have for their children. What is, of course, also necessary is that this family life can be characterised in acceptable ways, at least to those to the parents' social circle. In contemporary society this includes, in the language of case law, 'not foreclosing the child's options in later years'.

The Wollstonecraft–Godwin approach to domestic education could be interpreted in relation to EHE in the following way. A family that is well-functioning and outwardly facing, in terms of strong relationships with the broader community, expresses a particular view about how life ought to be lived. The purpose of education is to enable, and actively encouraged, the children to participate fully in the life of that family. In a society that values, as Western liberal democracies tend to, personal autonomy, a well-functioning family is one which lives out the tensions between personal freedoms and community life, and prepares the child to be able to make reasonable decisions about the kind of life they want to live. Where the child(ren) do attend school, this too is intended to support this educational narrative.

Approaches to EHE

The purpose of education does not, therefore, have to be set out in terms of 'learning outcomes'. Further, the institutional context of education is critical for both how it is conducted and how it is articulated; in this case either the family or the school. We see in Sutherland's analysis the ways in which the other institutions (friendships, chapel, literary groups, etc.) also give shape to specific approaches to education.

The formal–informal continuum is helpful in rejecting a dichotomy between informal and formal approaches to education. It is misleading, however, in two regards. The first, discussed earlier, is that it collapses the different dimensions one might be judging as formal–informal. The second is that it risks focussing attention on educational practices and ignoring the institutional characteristics within which education is occurring. Schools, especially, have a relatively universal, if phase specific, institutional structure and approach to education. Families on the other hand show a great deal of structural variation; they are unique expressions of particular sets of relationships. So, whilst there may be families similar to the Wollstonecraft–Godwin household in contemporary society, these are few, and will reflect the particular characteristics of the individuals in those families.

It is not surprising that EHE is expressed differently in different families, given that these families are themselves quite distinct, with a variety of ways in which they might be described on the formal–informal continuum. The choice between autonomous learning and more formal approaches is not a matter of 'pedagogy', understood as an analysis of methods, but of the particular beliefs a family has about itself, how children develop and how they are to be included in family life. The bias in EHE towards more autonomous forms of learning may not say so much about the 'naturalness' of such approaches, but the characteristics of families who can, and choose to, home educate. What does seem to emerge is the 'naturalness' of family life and the learning that occurs as children engage fully in that family life. What follows is that EHE researchers ought to focus more clearly not on the approaches to education per se, but on approaches to family life and the kinds of relationships between members of the family. (By extension, I think the same ought to direct work in other 'informal' education settings such as chapels and literary societies.)

As Kolodny (2010) points out, the characteristics of particular relationships between people emerge from the characteristics of the individual shared experiences of those people over time. So Godwin's relationship with his son with respect to school life is characterised by a particular history of family relationships and involvement in family life. This kind of analysis allows for a more considered reflection of the changing views of EHE practitioners over time. The experience of home educating shapes the relationship between parents, children and siblings, and itself comes to be part of the characterisation of family life. The approach to education, as to family life, is a fluid affair, in which parental dispositions, resources, context, broader community activity, and the experiences of children, and parents as home educators, combine in complex ways to direct EHE, and change it over the period the child is being home educated.

V. Conclusion

In drawing on the papers in this Special Issue I have explored the potential contribution they offer for EHE. The papers themselves cover the last era in the UK when education ideas and disputes were articulated without the perceived normalcy of the school. As such they represent a particular set of resources for EHE practitioners to think through their own practice without reference to the school. Following on from earlier work, I have drawn on 'upbringing' as a central justifying framework for the education of children. Education, whether conducted in the family or in school, ought to enable children to live better lives. The historical accounts, and the analysis of past educational practices, direct attention to both the purpose of, and approaches to, education. My focus has not been on exploring particular approaches to education, but the way in which such approaches can, and ought to be articulated.

In coming to a conclusion, I have argued that we ought to focus less on the characteristics of education and more on the characteristics of the family. This draws attention away from a schooling discourse on 'learning outcomes', towards a focus on the child learning through active engagement in the life of the family. The normative focus is on the kind of family which provides the context for a 'suitable education'. This is a politically sensitive arena as it *prioritises* questions about the nature and structure of families over the skills and abilities of parents as educators. It also raises differing accounts of 'pedagogy', rejecting a focus on method, for a concern with the character of the educator.

Alongside this argument for EHE practitioners (and researchers), I have offered some distinctions reflected in contemporary EHE practice which may be of interest to historians considering 'domestic pedagogies', in particular, distinctions between different accounts of pedagogy, practices and institutions, and different dimensions on the formal–informal continuum. These distinctions offered me an insight into the historical narratives presented. The value of these narratives for EHE is that they offer different perspectives on both 'domestic' and 'pedagogy', however, there are dangers in overstating *both* the similarity and dissimilarity. These distinctions, I hope, tread a line between both.

Acknowledgements

Thanks are due to Harriet Pattison, Rachael Davies, Evelyn Davies, Helen Lees and the reviewers for their comments on drafts of this paper.

Disclosure statement

No potential conflict of interest was reported by the author.

References

Badman, G. (2009). *Review into Elective Home Education in England*. London: TSO.

Biesta, G., Allan, J., & Edwards, R. (Eds.). (2014). *Making a difference in theory: The theory question in education and the education question in theory*. London: Routledge.

Darder, A., Baltodano, M. P., & Torres, R. D. (2009). *Critical pedagogy: An introduction*. New York: Routledge.

Davies, R. (2003). *Education, virtues and the good life: The ability of schools to inform and motivate students' moral behaviour* (Unpublished DPhil dissertation). University of Oxford, Oxford.

Davies, R. (2013a). After Higgins and Dunne: Imagining school teaching as a multi-practice activity. *Journal of Philosophy of Education, 43*, 475–490.

Davies, R. (2013b). Youth work, protest and a common language: Towards a framework for reasoned debate. *Youth and Policy, 110*, 52–65.

Davies, R. (2015). A suitable education? *Other Education, 4*, 16–32.

Department for Education (DfE). (2013). *Home–school agreements: Guidance for local authorities and governing bodies*. Retrieved from https://www.gov.uk/government/uploads/system/uploads/attachment_data/file/355588/home-school_agreement_guidance.pdf

Education Act. (1996). Retrieved from: http://www.legislation.gov.uk/ukpga/1997/44/contents

Gillard, D. (2011). *Education in England: A brief history*. Retrieved from: http://www.educationengland.org.uk/history

Hamilton, D. (1999). The pedagogic paradox (or why no didactics in England?). *Pedagogy, Culture & Society, 7*, 135–152.

Jeffs, T. & Smith, M. K. (1999). *Informal education: Conversation, democracy and learning*. Ticknall: Education Now.

Kolodny, N. (2010). Which relationships justify partiality? The case of parents and children. *Philosophy and Public Affairs, 38*, 37–75.

Lees, H. (2014). *Education without schools: Discovering alternatives*. Bristol: Policy Press.

MacIntyre, A. (1985). *After virtue* (2nd ed.). London: Duckworth.

MacIntyre, A. (1987). The idea of an educated public. In G. Haydon (Ed.), *Education and values: The Richard Peters lectures* (pp. 15–36). London: Institute of Education.

MacIntyre, A. (1999). *Dependent rational animals: Why human beings need the virtues*. Chicago: Open Court.

Morton, R. (2010). Home education: Constructions of choice. *International Electronic Journal of Elementary Education, 3*, 45–56.

Taylor, C. (1989). *Sources of the self: The making of modern identity*. Cambridge: Cambridge University Press.

Thomas, A. (1998). *Educating children at home*. London: Continuum.

Thomas, A. & Pattison, H. (2007). *How children learn at home*. E-book: Continuum.

United Nations (UN). (1989). *United Nations convention on the rights of the child*. Retrieved from http://www.ohchr.org/EN/ProfessionalInterest/Pages/CRC.aspx

Woolf, H. (1985). Mr Justice Woolf in the case of R v Secretary of State for Education and Science, ex parte Talmud Torah Machzikei Hadass School Trust (12 April 1985).

Index

accomplishments 17, 19, 32
ACE programme 116
active listening 31
advice literature 1, 12, 18, 30–31, 83–84, 90–91
agency 6
age segregation 6
Aikin, John 54
American Revolution 13–14
apprenticeships 72–75, 120
Arnold, Matthew 102
Arnold, Thomas 53
Ash, John 48
Astell, Mary 12
Austen, Jane 10, 16–22
autonomous learning 116

Barbauld, Anna Laetitia 54
Bennett, John 12–13, 45
Berquin, Arnaud 49
boarding schools 16–18, 22, 36, 45, 49–52
books, in working-class homes 66; *see also* literature
botany 36–37
boys: apprenticeships of 72–75, 120; education of 3, 5, 13, 28, 32, 45, 52
The Boys' School (Sandham) 56–57, 58
Broadhurst, Frances 45
Browning, Oscar 85
Brunton, Mary 21
Budden, Maria 48
Burney, Frances 18
Burr, Aaron 53–54
Burrows, Louie 104

Campbell, R. J. 108
Carey, John 48
Chambers, Jessie 104
chapels 106, 107–108
Chapone, Hester 13, 28
character development 52

child-centred learning 2
child psychology 83, 91
child-rearing, scientific approach to 90–93
children: relations between parents and 38; *see also* boys; girls
children's literature 2, 5, 44–58, 123; blending of public and private education and 51–57; domesticity and 46–51
Child Study movement 82–83, 91
Church, Lavinia 103, 106
circulating libraries 15
Clarion Clubs 108
class 45, 124–125; *see also* middle class; upper class; working class
classical curriculum 28, 32, 119–120
clerks, women 105–111
Clough, Anne Jemima 93–94
Cohen, Michele 11, 45
compulsory schooling 98–99, 114, 115
conduct literature 11–13, 28, 30–31, 57, 123
conversation 2, 6, 12, 27–39, 57; at home 29; skills 29–32
Corke, Helen 104–105
Cowper, William 28
criminal records 62–78
criminal skills 76–77
critical judgement 31
critical pedagogies 121–122
The Crofton Boys (Martineau) 55
culture: conversation and 28; oral 31
cumulative talk 35
curriculum: classical 28, 32; core 32; liberal 82; online 116

Darwin, Erasmus 45
Day, Thomas 47–48
Defoe, Daniel 17–18, 49, 119
demographic change 6
dialogic texts 32–39
discipline 94
domestic education *see* home education

INDEX

domesticity, children's literature and 46–51
domestic pedagogies 1–2, 10–23, 117–122, 124
domestic realism 49
du Boscq, Jacques 22

Edgeworth, Maria 47–53, 56, 84, 119
Edgeworth, Richard Lowell 52, 84
education 13; agency in 6; of boys 3, 5, 13, 28, 32, 45, 52; contemporary conceptions of 7; debate over public vs. private 10–22, 44–58, 123; definition of 115; disciplinary functions of 20–21; formal/informal dichotomy 98–112, 123, 124, 126; of girls 11–12, 28, 32, 45, 118–119; history of 11; individualised 56–57; institutions vs. practices 123–124; of lower middle class women 98–112; purpose of 122–126; in working-class homes 62–78; *see also* home education; school education
Education Act (1870) 66
Education Act (1944) 114, 115
Education Act (1996) 115
educational theory, of eighteenth century 11–12
Edwardian Britain 98–112
eighteenth century: debate over public or private education in 10–22, 44–58; familiar conversation in 27–39; gender roles in 11, 15–16
eighteenth-century novel, home education of girls in 10–23
Elective Home Education (EHE) 2, 6, 114–127
elementary schooling: nationwide system of 2; religiously sponsored 65
elite *see* upper class
Emile (Rousseau) 12
Emma (Austen) 16–17
Enlightenment theory 6
equal pay 103
Essex, John 12
Evelina (Burney) 18
Evenings at Home (Aikin and Barbauld) 54

familiar conversations 27–39
family culture 1
family/families: as institution 123–124; literacy skills and 66–67; middle class 3, 5, 6, 14–15, 46, 86–88, 92–93, 98–112; upper class 3, 6, 46, 86–88, 93, 118–119, 125; women in lower middle class 98–112; working class 3–5, 62–78, 100, 119–120, 124–125
family life 6, 54; changes in 14–15; learning from 114–115

family size 6, 89
Fanshaw, Althea 54–55
Farington, Joseph 44–45
fathers 45, 47, 66, 71, 72–73, 88; *see also* parents
female education 3, 5–7, 10–23, 28, 32, 45, 118–119
Female Quixote (Lennox) 18–19
femininity 15–16, 21, 45
feminism 103, 108
Fenn, Ellenor 47, 48, 52
Fergus, Jan 56
Fielding, Sarah 56
Fleming, Selina 85
formal/informal education dichotomy 98–112, 123, 124, 126
Forster Act 2
French Revolution 14
friendship, within family 6

gender 6–7; in eighteenth century 11, 15–16; home education and 99–100, 118–119
girls: boarding schools for 45; education of 3, 5–7, 10–23, 28, 32, 45, 118–119
Gisborne, Thomas 13
Godwin, William 10, 15, 53–54, 57, 118, 121–122, 125

Hardy, Thomas 101, 107
Hays, Mary 16
Haywood, Eliza 17
Helme, Elizabeth 37, 38
The History of Miss Betsy Thoughtless (Haywood) 17
Home and Colonial School Society (HCSS) Training College 82
home education: for boys 3, 32, 45; Charlotte Mason and 81–95; children's literature and 46–51; continuity between school and 51–57; current state of 115–117; definition of 4–5; in eighteenth-century literature 16–22; elective 2, 6, 114–127; familiar conversation format and 27–39; gender and 6–7, 99–100; for girls 3, 6–7, 10–23, 32, 118–119; introduction to 1–7; lower middle class and 98–112; occupational skills and 71–75; vs. public education 10–22, 44–58, 123; in working-class homes 62–78, 119–120
Home Education (Mason) 81, 82–86, 88
homeschooling 4
Hoxton Adult School 108

Inchbald, Elizabeth 10, 16, 20, 21
institutional instruction 1, 2, 87, 94, 106; *see also* school education

INDEX

institutions vs. practices 123–124
intergenerational exchange 6
Ipswich County Goal records 62–78

Johnson, Alan 103
Jones, Hugh 109
Jude the Obscure (Hardy) 101, 107
juvenile publishing 32

Kilner, Dorothy 50
knowledge: body of 119; specialisation of 3
Knox, Vicesimus 12

Lafitte, Francoise 109
language socialisation 30
Lawrence, D. H. 103–104, 111
learning outcomes 125, 126
Lennox, Charlotte 18–19
liberal curriculum 82
libraries 15, 32, 106–107
literacy rates/skills 2, 65–71
literature: advice 1, 12, 18, 30–31, 83–84, 90–91; children's 2, 5, 44–58, 123; conduct 11–13, 28, 30–31, 57, 123; domestic pedagogies in 10–23
'living ideas' 83
Locke, John 11, 31

manners 30
Mansfield Park (Austen) 18, 19–21
Marcet, Jane 36
marriage 18, 101
Martineau, Harriet 45, 55
masculinity 45
Mason, Charlotte 3, 81–95, 121–122
mass schooling 4
media 15
Memoirs of Emma Courtney (Hays) 16
memory 31
middle class 3, 5–6, 14–15, 46, 86–88, 92–93, 98–112
Mill, John Stuart 45
Moll Flanders (Defoe) 17–18, 119
Monro, Alexander 12
More, Hannah 13, 21
mothers 6, 47, 71, 82–83, 88–89, 91–92, 121; *see also* parents
Mothers' Education Course (MEC) 84–85, 91, 119

national character 3
National Home Reading Union 4
National Union of Teachers 103
natural learning 20, 116
Newbery, John 46
newpapers 15

The New Robinson Crusoe (Defoe) 49, 50
New Theology 108
night schools 105–106
nineteenth century 1–2; criminal records from 62–78; debate over public or private education in 44–58; familiar conversation in 27–39
Normal School 100, 101

occupational instruction 4, 7, 71–75, 122
online programmes 116
oral culture 31

parents: conversation with 35; literacy skills and 67; middle class 92–93; relations between children and 38; role of 2, 7, 20, 52, 82–83, 93, 114; as teachers 28, 71; training of 90–92, 121; upper class 93; *see also* fathers; mothers
Parents' National Educational Union (PENU) 81–95, 99; appeal of 87, 90–94; clientele of 86–90; origins of 82–86
Parents' Review 87–89, 91–92, 93
Parents' Union School 95
pedagogy: of conversation 27–39; critical pedagogies 121–122; domestic pedagogies 1, 2, 10–23, 117–122, 124; meaning of 120–122
poaching 77
politeness 31, 37, 39
political organisations 108–109
polytechnics 106
power 6–7
preparatory schools 86
prison records 62–78
private education 4
private sphere 11, 22
Progressive Thought League 108
public libraries 106–107
public moralism 6
public sphere 11
Pullen, Henry William 45
pupil-teachers 100–105

questions 29, 31

reading aloud 31
reading skills 70–71
Regency novels 11
religious institutions 3, 65, 107–108
Romantic fiction 2
rote learning 35
Rousseau, Jean-Jacques 11, 12, 20, 84
Runciman, James 101–102

INDEX

Sadler, Michael 85
'Salt Hill' 57
Sandham, Elizabeth 56–57, 58
school education: in children's literature 49–51; compulsory 98–99, 114, 115; continuity between home and 51–57; expansion of 86, 94; vs. home education 10–22, 44–58; need for 3; preparation of children for 92–93
schools: data on nineteenth-century 70; night 105–106; polytechnics 106; preparatory 86; working class 3–4
Schools Inquiry Commission 39
school stories 49–52, 55–57
secondary schooling, nationwide system of 2
self-education 3, 5, 31, 68, 98–112
self-improvement 4, 5
separate spheres 15
Shirreff, Emily 85
Shteir, Ann 36–37
Simmons, Minna 109–110
A Simple Story (Inchbald) 10, 16, 20, 21
Slate, Ruth 105–111
Slawson, Eva 105–111
sociability 2, 3, 6, 28, 37, 39
social norms 119
society, role of women in 3, 11, 14–15, 22
Spencer, F. H. 102
suffrage movement 103, 107, 109

teachers 51; parents as 28, 71; professional 19–20, 93; training of 82, 85; women maintained school teachers 100–105
teachers' union 103
teaching, professionalisation of 3, 85
Thomson, David 109, 110
Trimmer, Sarah 47

University Extension Movement 85, 102, 103
unschooling 4
upbringing 122–124
upper class 3, 6, 46, 86–88, 93, 118–119, 125

Walker, George 49
Watkins, Lucy 50
West, Jane 21
white-collar jobs 99–111, 119–120
Wollstonecraft, Mary 12, 13, 15, 22, 35, 48, 53, 119, 121–123, 125
women: clerks 105–111; lower middle class 98–112; middle class 14–15; in society 3, 11, 14–15, 22; white-collar work for 99–111, 119–120
women maintained school teachers 100–105
Woodley, Sophia 10–11
work ethic 71
working class 3–5, 100, 124–125; criminal skills of 76–77; home education of 62–78, 119–120; literacy skills of 65–71; occupational skills of 71–75
World Wide Education Service 95
writing skills 70–71